THE COMPLETE BOOK OF
SALADS

THE COMPLETE BOOK OF

SALADS

ALESSANDRA AVALLONE

Photographs by
Franco Pizzochero

GALLERY BOOKS
An imprint of W.H. Smith Publishers Inc.
112 Madison Avenue
New York, New York 10016

Published in the US by Gallery Books, an imprint owned by
W.H. Smith Publishers, Inc.
112 Madison Avenue
New York, New York 10016

Translated from the Italian by
Elaine Hardy
Additional material translated by
Chrissa Woodhouse
Copyright © 1988 Arnoldo Mondadori
Editore S.p.A Milan
English translation copyright ©
1989 Arnoldo Mondadori Editore
S.p.A., Milan

ISBN 0-8317-7669-2

Printed and bound in Italy by Arnoldo Mondadori Editore, Verona

Note: Measurements are given in metric,
imperial and, where relevant, US cups.
Follow one system only.

CONTENTS

For my mother and my sister

FOREWORD

For many years salads have tended to play a secondary role in the culinary world. Recent trends towards healthier eating, however, together with the increasingly pressurized lifestyle of the working cook have resulted in a reappraisal of the formerly humble salad.

At last the salad has been brought to the fore, often appearing alone as a substantial main course. An enormous range of locally grown and more exotic basic ingredients is now widely available and can be combined in the most varied and imaginative ways to suit all kinds of meals, from an elegant dinner party or gourmet supper to an informal lunch or simple vegetarian snack.

Appealing both to the waistline as well as to the palate, salads are always a guaranteed success, easy and quick to prepare with very few golden rules. Imagination is perhaps the most important ingredient and the one this book seeks to promote.

The first rule is to aim for a well-balanced dish in terms of flavour, texture and colour. Where several ingredients are used no single one should predominate. For example if you are including a particularly strong ingredient make sure it does not overpower more delicately flavoured ones.

The second rule is to choose the right dressing. Oil and vinegar are used as the basis of most condiments, but even of these two simple ingredients infinite varieties exist; learning to select the most suitable will enable you to transform an otherwise ordinary recipe into a new and exciting dish. Finally, we see how herbs and spices can add that special touch of freshness and fragrance with a new look to suit every occasion.

INTRODUCTION

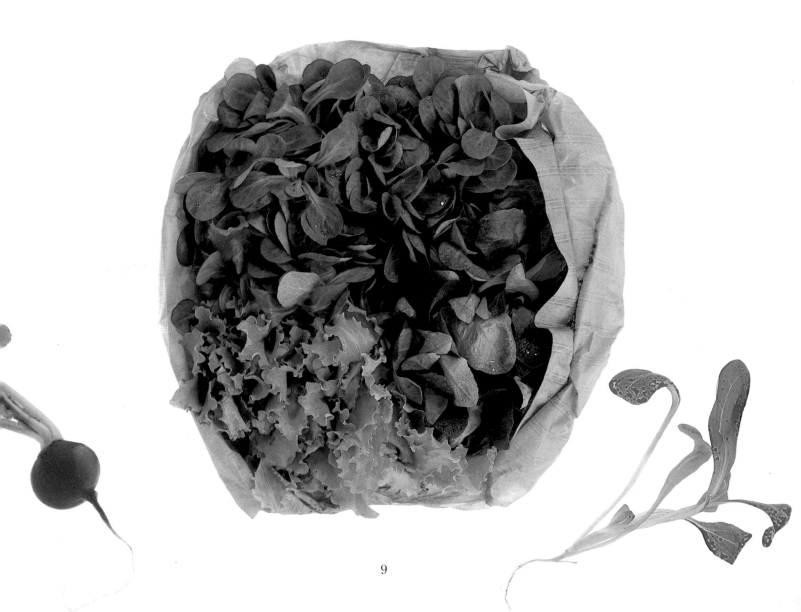

maize oil   walnut oil   extra virgin olive oil   sage and rosemary oil   myrtle oil

OIL

Oil is a liquid vegetable fat extracted from a wide range of fruits, nuts and seeds. Oils extracted from peanuts, sunflower seeds and maize are not suitable for dressing salads as they have little or no flavour. Walnut and hazelnut oils, on the other hand, have a unique and delicate flavour that is ideal for certain salads. Typical of certain regions such as Provence, they are unfortunately very expensive and do not keep for more than a couple of months. When they are available, it is only worth buying a small, usable quantity at a time.

An entire book could be devoted to the merits of olive oil which provides the basis of any good salad dressing. Always use extra virgin olive oil since this is the only oil obtained from the first

garlic oil   fennel oil   bay leaf and allspice oil   chilli oil   thyme oil

mechanical (as opposed to chemical) cold pressing, and its characteristic good qualities are therefore preserved. From a nutritional point of view olive oil is excellent thanks to its low oleic acid content; above all it has a rich and full flavour.

Olive oil varies in strength, flavour and colour from pale to dark green.

Like vinegar, oil can also be flavoured with herbs and spices. Examples include:

1 Chilli oil for meat, vegetable, pasta and rice salads.
2 Garlic oil for tomato and green salads.
3 Sage and rosemary oil for cooked vegetable, meat or fish salads.
4 Fennel oil for fish, shellfish and cheese salads.
5 Pepper-flavoured oil for all salads.
6 Allspice oil for cheese and savoury/sweet salads.
7 Oregano and marjoram oil for summer and pasta salads.
8 Bay or thyme oil for meat and cheese salads.
9 Myrtle oil for meat and cheese salads and many others you may want to try.

| champagne vinegar with pink peppercorns | tarragon champagne vinegar | shallot white wine vinegar | cider vinegar | paprika, bay leaf and coriander white wine vinegar |

VINEGAR

Vinegar is a by-product of the acetous fermentation that takes place in alcoholic substrates of certain liquids when a specific group of bacteria is present. Different vinegars can be obtained according to the alcohol used:

cider, malt, rice wine, sherry, white wine, red wine, champagne etc. The most common in the West is wine vinegar, one of the basic ingredients of the classic vinaigrette.

If the wine is of good quality, the vinegar obtained will have a pronounced flavour and distinct perfume. It will enliven any dressing and enhance the flavour of every ingredient. If you want to add a really special touch to your salads, you can prepare a selection of your own vinegars by adding your favourite herbs, spices and fruit flavourings.

The basic recipe is extremely simple: choose very fresh herbs or fruit, preferably just picked

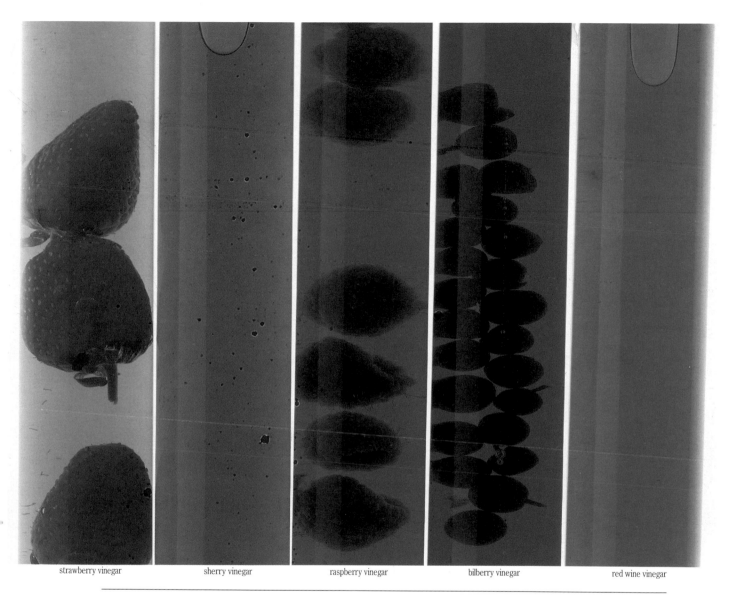

| strawberry vinegar | sherry vinegar | raspberry vinegar | bilberry vinegar | red wine vinegar |

if possible. Wash them carefully and place them in a bottle of vinegar. Seal the bottle so that it is airtight and leave it in a dark place for three to four weeks. Filter the amount required through a fine piece of muslin or coffee filter paper. Hermetically seal the rest and store in a cool dark place. Here is a list of the most typical combinations to which you can add others of your choice:

1 Shallot and garlic red wine vinegar for meat, tomato and green salads.
2 Green pepper and red pepper red wine vinegar for fish and meat salads.
3 Pink peppercorn champagne vinegar for savoury/sweet salads and light salads with flowers.
4 Mint red wine vinegar for salads with meat, shellfish, seafood, courgettes (zucchini) etc.
5 Tarragon champagne vinegar for fish, beansprouts and green salads.
6 Strawberry white wine vinegar for savoury/sweet and fruit salads.
7 Raspberry (and other fruits of the forest) white wine vinegar for savoury/sweet, meat and game salads or salads with flowers or beansprouts.
8 Coriander, chilli, bay leaf and pepper vinegar for exotic and spicy salads.

MAIN COURSE SALADS

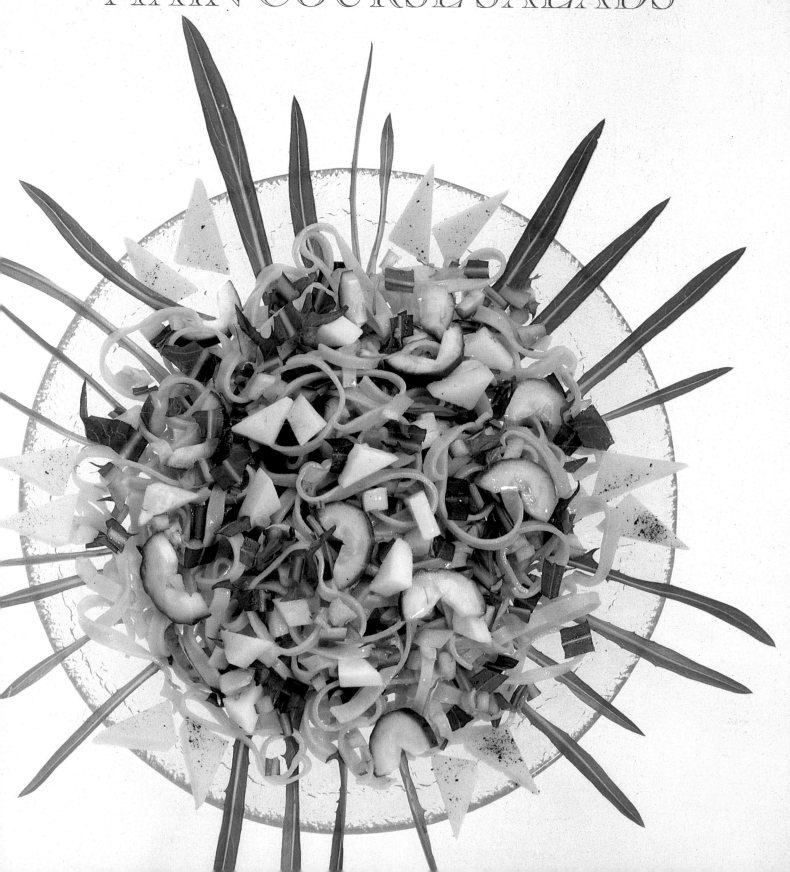

The classic complete meal may typically include an appetizer, first course, main course with vegetable accompaniment, dessert, cheese and fruit. Although it is entertaining to think up such a menu, there are few of us who have not occasionally worried about the time and calories involved, not to mention the toll on our digestion. We are simply not used to eating such great amounts on a day-to-day basis, and the one-course meal is quite often the most practical solution. This need not mean, however, that it is any less interesting; the challenge of producing a dish that is well-balanced both in terms of ingredients and nutritional value can lead to the creation of an infinite variety of new ideas. Farinaceous products such as pasta, rice, pulses, potatoes and even bread are excellent for this kind of dish, often forming a substantial, fairly neutral base which can be enhanced and complemented by the stronger flavours and textures of meat, fish, cheese or vegetables. Requiring virtually no advance preparation, main course salads involve little or no cooking and are therefore ideal for the busy cook.

On the previous page:
Saffron pasta salad

SAFFRON PASTA SALAD

Serves 4

1 head chicory (Belgian endive)

2 cucumbers

300 g/10 oz Provolone cheese

salt and freshly ground black pepper

extra virgin olive oil

1 tsp fennel seeds

1 clove garlic

red wine vinegar

2 shallots

1 bunch parsley

1 strip green pepper

6 gherkins

1 envelope saffron powder

300 g/10 oz/2 cups pasta rings

Rinse the chicory (Belgian endive) under cold running water, drain then tear coarsely. Wash and dry the cucumbers. Using an apple corer remove and discard the seeds from the middle. Cut in half lengthwise, then slice. Cut the cheese into dice, then into triangles. Place all the ingredients in a large bowl and season with pepper and 2 tbsp olive oil. Make the dressing: pound the fennel seeds and peeled garlic clove using a mortar and pestle. Add 2 tbsp vinegar and a few tbsp oil; chop the shallots, parsley, green pepper and gherkins and add to the dressing. Season with salt and pepper. Pour the saffron powder into a large saucepan of salted water and bring to the boil. Add 1 tbsp oil, then add the pasta and cook for 10–12 minutes or until *al dente* (tender, but retaining some bite). Drain the pasta and run under cold water. Add to the other ingredients in the bowl, pour over the dressing, mix well and leave to stand for 30 minutes before serving.

Pasta salad all'italiana

PASTA SALAD ALL'ITALIANA

Serves 4

6 dried tomatoes

1 dried red chilli pepper

1 tsp oregano

extra virgin olive oil

salt and freshly ground black pepper

4 ripe tomatoes

300 g/10 oz romanesco or broccoli

300 g/10 oz/2 cups pasta quills

250 g/9 oz ricotta

12 black olives

1 onion

Finely chop the dried tomatoes and chilli pepper. Add the oregano and 6 tbsp oil. Season with salt and pepper and leave to stand while you prepare the other ingredients. Wash and dry the 4 tomatoes and sprinkle with salt. Wash the romanesco, break into florets and cook in boiling water for 10 minutes. Remove the florets with a slotted spoon and cook the pasta in the same water for 10–12 minutes. Drain and pass under cold running water. Mix together in a bowl the pasta, tomatoes, romanesco, crumbled ricotta, olives and finely chopped onion. Pour over the chilli dressing and adjust the seasoning. Chill for 1 hour before serving.
Note: Romanesco is a hybrid variety of cauliflower. If unavailable, substitute broccoli.

HERRING SALAD

Serves 4

300 g/10 oz rollmops

3 large gherkins

300 g/10 oz boiled potatoes

150 g/5 oz cooked beetroot

3 hard-boiled eggs

150 ml/5 fl oz/⅔ cup natural yoghurt

1 tbsp lemon juice

1 clove garlic, chopped

salt and freshly ground black pepper

2 tbsp chopped dill

Unroll the herrings and cut into 1-cm/½-in pieces. Slice the gherkins. Dice the potatoes and beetroot. Shell the eggs and chop coarsely, then place all these ingredients in a bowl. Mix together the yoghurt, lemon juice and garlic; season with salt and pepper, pour over the salad and sprinkle with the chopped dill. Serve well chilled.

———

PASTA SALAD JARDINIÈRE

Serves 4

1 large courgette (zucchini)

1 carrot

1 small head fennel

100 g/4 oz cocktail onions

200 g/7 oz broccoli

150 g/5 oz/1 cup frozen peas

extra virgin olive oil

salt and freshly ground black pepper

400 g/14 oz/2½ cups wholewheat pasta shapes

1 small cooked beetroot

2 tomatoes

1 red onion

1 small bunch lemon balm

few chives (optional)

1 tbsp vinegar

1 tbsp lemon juice

Wash and trim all the vegetables. Cut the large ones into dice and chop the rest. Cook together for 5 minutes in boiling water the courgette (zucchini), carrot, fennel, onions, broccoli and peas. Drain and sauté in 3 tbsp oil. Season with salt and pepper.

Pasta salad jardinière

Cook the pasta in boiling salted water for 10–12 minutes until *al dente*, then pass under cold water to stop the cooking process. Add the sautéed vegetables, diced beetroot, the seeded and chopped tomatoes, the chopped onion and chopped herbs. When the pasta is cold, mix all ingredients and dress with a vinaigrette of vinegar, lemon juice, 4 tbsp oil, salt and pepper.

SPICY HAM AND TURKEY SALAD

Serves 4

1 yellow pepper
1 red pepper
200 g/7 oz cooked ham, in one slice
200 g/7 oz cooked turkey meat
1 carton beansprouts
1 bunch parsley
salt and freshly ground black pepper
extra virgin olive oil
1 tbsp mustard
red wine vinegar
300 g/10 oz/2 cups pasta bows

Rinse the peppers. Cut in half, remove the seeds, then slice. Reserve a few strips for garnish and chop the rest. Cut off any fat from the ham and turkey and dice the meat. Place these ingredients in a bowl and add the chopped parsley and beansprouts. Sprinkle with pepper and 2 tbsp oil. Mix the mustard with 2 tbsp vinegar, then gradually beat in 5–6 tbsp oil. Cook the pasta for 10–12 minutes in boiling salted water until *al dente*. Drain and cool under running water before adding to the other ingredients. Pour over the mustard dressing, season with salt and pepper and leave to stand for a while before serving.

Spicy ham and turkey salad

AUBERGINE (EGGPLANT) AND LAMB SALAD

Serves 4

1 bunch mint

2 slices white bread, crusts removed

vinegar

200 g/7 oz ground lamb

1 egg

salt and freshly ground black pepper

flour

extra virgin olive oil

2 small aubergines (eggplant)

1 small head curly lettuce

200 ml/7 fl oz/scant 1 cup natural yoghurt

2 tbsp single (light) cream

1 clove garlic, chopped

1 tbsp chopped onion

Rinse and trim the mint, then chop coarsely. Break up the bread and moisten with 1 tbsp vinegar. Mix together in a bowl the ground lamb, bread, egg, 2 tbsp chopped mint, salt and pepper. Shape the mixture into walnut-sized balls, flour lightly, then fry in hot oil. Drain on kitchen paper and keep warm. Rinse, trim and peel the aubergines (eggplant); cut into dice and place in a colander. Sprinkle with salt and leave to stand for 1 hour, to drain off the bitter juices. Rinse and pat dry. Fry in hot oil until golden brown. Drain on kitchen paper and sprinkle with salt. Rinse the lettuce and tear into pieces with your hands. Mix together in a bowl the yoghurt and cream, the garlic, chopped onion and remaining mint. Season with salt and pepper. Just before serving, mix together the lettuce, lamb balls and aubergines (eggplant). Serve the yoghurt sauce separately.

POTATO SALAD NORMANDE

Serves 4

600 g/1¼ lb new potatoes

salt and freshly ground black pepper

cider vinegar

extra virgin olive oil

300 g/10 oz smoked ham

1 head white celery

1 small red apple

½ tsp coarse grain mustard

½ tsp honey

1 clove garlic, crushed

2 tbsp chopped parsley

Scrub the potatoes thoroughly to remove any earth but do not peel. Cook in boiling salted water for about 15 minutes or until tender. Drain and leave to cool. Cut into slices and sprinkle with 2 tbsp vinegar and 3 tbsp oil. Dice the ham. Rinse the celery, discarding the tougher sticks, and slice the rest including the leaves. Chop the red apple. Mix together in a bowl the mustard, honey and crushed garlic. Add 4 tbsp vinegar and 10 tbsp oil and season with salt and pepper. Mix together in a large bowl the potatoes, ham, celery and red apple. Dress with a little of the sauce, sprinkle with the parsley, and leave to stand for 30 minutes before serving. Serve the remaining sauce separately.

SALADE NIÇOISE

Serves 4

1 lettuce

4 tomatoes

1 small cucumber

12 black olives

4 hard-boiled eggs

½ red pepper

2 shallots
400 g/14 oz canned tuna in oil
red wine vinegar
extra virgin olive oil
salt and freshly ground black pepper
2 cloves garlic
200 g/7 oz cooked French beans
8 slices French bread

Rinse the lettuce and tear coarsely with your hands. Cut the tomatoes into wedges; peel and dice the cucumber. Pit the olives and cut in half. Shell and quarter the eggs and coarsely chop the pepper. Slice the shallots, then drain and flake the tuna. Arrange on a serving platter or distribute the ingredients evenly between 4 individual bowls. Make a vinaigrette by combining 3 tbsp vinegar, 6 tbsp oil, salt, pepper and 1 chopped clove garlic. Pour over the salad. Toast the slices of bread and rub with the remaining cut clove of garlic. Sprinkle lightly with pepper and serve with the salad.

PASTA AND SMOKED MACKEREL SALAD

Serves 4
300 g/10 oz smoked mackerel
salt and freshly ground black pepper
juice of 1 lemon
1 green apple
1 celery heart
1 head fennel
150 ml/5 fl oz/$\frac{2}{3}$ cup mayonnaise
150 ml/5 fl oz/$\frac{2}{3}$ cup single (light) cream
1 tbsp freshly grated horseradish
300 g/10 oz/2 cups pasta shapes
extra virgin olive oil

Remove the skin from the mackerel, flake into pieces with a fork and season with pepper and 1 tbsp lemon juice. Peel the apple, discard the core, then dice and sprinkle immediately with lemon juice to prevent discoloration. Trim and rinse the celery and fennel and slice both. Mix the mayonnaise with the cream and remaining lemon juice; add the horseradish and season with salt and pepper. Cook the pasta in boiling salted water for 10–12 minutes or until *al dente* (tender, but retaining some bite). Drain and pass under cold running water. Leave to cool completely, then season with 2 tbsp oil. Mix together in a large bowl the mackerel, pasta, vegetables and apple. Pour over the dressing and mix thoroughly.

CABBAGE AND FRANKFURTER SALAD

Serves 4

1 cabbage

½ tsp cumin seeds

salt and freshly ground black pepper

vinegar

4 large frankfurters

150 g/5 oz lean smoked bacon

extra virgin olive oil

Discard the tough outer leaves of the cabbage and finely shred the rest. Rinse and dry thoroughly. Pound the cumin seeds with a pestle and mortar and sprinkle over the cabbage with 2 pinches of salt and pepper. Sprinkle with 3 tbsp vinegar and leave to stand for 1 hour. Shortly before serving, boil the frankfurters, then slice. Dice the bacon and fry briefly in 2 tbsp oil. Add the hot bacon and frankfurters to the cabbage, mix thoroughly and serve.

SEAFOOD SALAD

Serves 4

1 kg/2¼ lb mussels

1 glass white wine

24 prawns (shrimp)

600 g/1¼ lb baby octopus

2 tsp lemon juice

salt and freshly ground black pepper

extra virgin olive oil

2 large bunches rocket

200 g/7 oz long-grain rice

2 cloves garlic

1 shallot

1 spring onion (scallion)

1 bunch dill

Seafood salad

2 ripe tomatoes
300 ml/10 fl oz/1¼ cups single (light) cream
½ tsp tomato purée

Scrub the mussels thoroughly under running water and remove the beards and barnacles. Discard any that do not close when tapped sharply. Place in a large saucepan with the white wine and cook over high heat for a few minutes until the shells open. Discard any that remain closed. Strain and reserve the liquor. Remove the mussels from their shells. Simmer the prawns (shrimp) in the liquor for 5 minutes. Drain and shell the prawns (shrimp), setting aside 4 tbsp of the cooking liquid; add 1 liter/1¾ pints/4½ cups hot water to the rest and cook the baby octopus for about 45 minutes or until tender. Place all the seafood in a bowl and sprinkle with half the lemon juice, pepper, 3 tbsp oil and salt to taste. Wash and trim the rocket; chop coarsely and add to the seafood. Cook the rice in boiling water according to the manufacturer's instructions. When tender, drain and rinse under cold water. Add to the other ingredients and chill in the refrigerator for at least 1 hour. Chop the garlic, shallot, spring onion (scallion) including the green part, and the dill. Blanch the tomatoes for 1 minute in boiling water, then peel them, discard the seeds and slice. Heat the reserved 4 tbsp liquor in a small saucepan until reduced to 1 tbsp. Add the cream and tomato purée. Simmer until it begins to thicken, then sprinkle with pepper. Adjust the seasoning, add the lemon juice, chopped herbs and onions, and the tomatoes. Serve the seafood salad cold with the warmed sauce.

PAN BAGNÁ

Serves 4
2 cloves garlic
1 tsp Dijon mustard
salt and freshly ground black pepper
cider vinegar

extra virgin olive oil

1 French stick

4 ripe tomatoes

1 onion

2 tbsp pitted olives

8 anchovy fillets in oil

1 small pepper

This substantial tomato, onion and olive sandwich is a traditional French snack which is ideal for a picnic or midday summer meal. Peel the garlic and crush with the blade of a large knife. Place in a bowl with the mustard, salt and pepper; add 3 tbsp vinegar and 6 tbsp oil and beat with a small whisk to make a vinaigrette. Cut the French stick in half lengthwise without cutting right through, open it and sprinkle with the vinaigrette. On top of one half only place the tomatoes, cut into slices; the onion, sliced in rings; the chopped olives; the anchovies; and the pepper, sliced with seeds removed. Close the French stick, wrap in foil, then place a weight along the entire length and leave to stand for 30 minutes. Cut into 4 equal parts to serve.

SPAGHETTI SALAD WITH RADICCHIO

Serves 4

4 eggs

1 tbsp chopped onion

2 tbsp chopped parsley

salt and freshly ground black pepper

extra virgin olive oil

2 heads radicchio

10 thin slices salami

300 g/10 oz spaghetti (or linguine)

150 g/5 oz/1¼ cups sweetcorn

chilli powder (optional)

1 clove garlic

Break the eggs into a bowl and beat in the onion, chopped parsley, salt and pepper. Heat 1 tbsp oil in a non-stick frying pan; make an omelette, leave to cool, then cut into strips. Rinse and slice the radicchio. Cut the salami into thin strips. Cook the spaghetti in boiling salted water for 10–12 minutes or until *al dente* (tender, but retaining some bite), then rinse under cold running water. While still warm mix with the chicory, sweetcorn, salami and omelette strips. Sprinkle with black pepper, chilli powder (if using), chopped garlic and salt. Dress with olive oil and serve at once.

BEAN AND TOMATO SALAD

Serves 4

1 head radicchio or lollo rosso

1 heart escarole

400 g/14 oz/1¼ cups cooked borlotti beans

salt and freshly ground black pepper

few chives

1 bunch spring onions (scallions)

10 basil leaves

250 g/9 oz tomatoes

1 bunch parsley

red wine vinegar

extra virgin olive oil flavoured with garlic

Rinse and trim the lettuces and shred. Sprinkle the beans with salt and plenty of pepper, chopped chives and spring onions (scallions) and the torn basil leaves. Slice the tomatoes, add to the other ingredients, and transfer to a serving bowl or platter. Mix well and leave to stand in a cool place for a few hours. Chop the parsley. Dress the salad with the flavoured oil and vinegar, and sprinkle with parsley.

Spaghetti salad with radicchio

LAST MINUTE SALADS

Friends turn up unexpectedly and stay for supper; an impromptu celebration; a quick snack before the cinema – how many times have you been called upon to produce a meal at the last minute, without having included the ingredients with the day's shopping? With a well-stocked larder and a few leftovers in the refrigerator it is quite simple to come up with a dish that will spare you the usual standby measures. This chapter includes recipes using products which are either frozen or canned, or simple, fresh ingredients that would be routinely kept in most kitchens. Look around, see what there is and mix it all together to create a salad. Without wishing to deny the superiority of fresh foods over frozen and canned goods, it is nevertheless extremely useful to keep in stock a small supply of certain ingredients for emergencies. Purists who balk at the thought can always use their own preserves and frozen goods.

On the previous page:
Chicory salad with Bresaola

CHICORY SALAD WITH BRESAOLA

Serves 4

1 small frisée lettuce or escarole

4 heads chicory (Belgian endive)

250 g/9 oz Bresaola

juice of 1 lemon

salt and freshly ground black pepper

extra virgin olive oil

Trim and rinse the lettuce and tear into pieces. Rinse the chicory (Belgian endive), discard the bitter central core, then slice. Cut the Bresaola into thin strips and pour over a dressing made by beating together the lemon juice, salt and pepper, and 6 tbsp oil. Leave to stand for 10 minutes, then transfer the Bresaola and dressing into a bowl with the salad. Mix thoroughly and sprinkle generously with pepper before serving.
Note: Bresaola is a paper-thin dried salt beef. If unavailable, substitute a similar cured beef.

POTATO AND RED ONION SALAD

Serves 4

1 small jar (about 125 g/4 oz) pickled vegetables

1 tbsp coarse grain mustard

red wine or sherry vinegar

extra virgin olive oil flavoured with thyme

2 red onions

800 g/1¾ lb new potatoes

1 bunch parsley

salt and freshly ground black pepper

Chop the pickled vegetables, then mix with the mustard,

Potato and red onion salad

Carrot and palm heart salad

3–4 tbsp vinegar and 100 ml/3½ fl oz/scant ½ cup oil. Finely slice the onions into rings, add to the dressing and leave to stand for 30 minutes. Scrub the potatoes clean, then cook in boiling salted water for about 15 minutes or until tender. Cut them into cubes but do not peel; pour over the dressing while they are still hot and sprinkle with plenty of parsley, salt and pepper. Mix thoroughly before serving.

SALAD WITH MEATBALLS AND CELERY

Serves 4

300 g/10 oz/1¼ cups ground beef

2 slices white bread, dipped in milk and squeezed out

40 g/1½ oz/¾ cup grated Parmesan

1 clove garlic, chopped

1 bunch fresh basil or parsley

grated nutmeg

salt and freshly ground black pepper

1 egg

plain (all-purpose) flour

200 g/7 oz mixed lettuce

1 celery heart

oil for frying

sherry vinegar

extra virgin olive oil

Mix together the ground beef, soaked and crumbled bread, Parmesan, garlic, 2 tbsp chopped fresh herbs, 2 pinches grated nutmeg, salt and pepper. Mix in the egg, and shape into meatballs the size of a large walnut. Coat lightly in flour. Trim and rinse the salad and tear into pieces, then rinse and coarsely chop the celery. Fry the meatballs in hot oil until golden brown, drain on kitchen paper, then add to the salad. Dress with vinegar, olive oil, salt and pepper and stir carefully before serving.

CARROT AND PALM HEART SALAD

Serves 4

450 g/1 lb carrots

1 can palm hearts

50 g/2 oz/¼ cup roasted peanuts

1½ tsp capers

salt and freshly ground black pepper

juice of 1 lemon

walnut oil

chopped dill (fresh or dried)

Trim and peel the carrots, then slice into matchsticks using a mandoline cutter, or grate them into a large bowl. Add the drained and halved palm hearts, half the peanuts and half the capers. Season with salt and pepper, sprinkle with the lemon juice, a few tbsp walnut oil and plenty of dill. Leave to stand for 10 minutes, stirring occasionally. Add the remaining whole capers and peanuts before serving. For a spicier dressing, make the vinaigrette with 1 tsp strong mustard, 2 tbsp vinegar, a pinch of ground ginger, oil and plenty of salt and pepper.

POTATO SALAD WITH COTTAGE CHEESE AND HERBS

Serves 4

400 g/14 oz/2 cups plain cottage cheese

2 tbsp double (heavy) cream

salt and freshly ground black pepper

1 bunch fresh (or dried) mixed herbs (e.g. parsley, basil, mint, tarragon, celery and fennel leaves)

2 hard-boiled eggs

strawberry vinegar

extra virgin olive oil flavoured with garlic

600 g/1¼ lb cooked potatoes

Drain the cottage cheese, and mix with the cream and a pinch of salt and pepper. Finely chop the herbs and shell the eggs. Chop the eggs, then mash with a fork before adding the chopped herbs, salt and pepper, 3 tbsp strawberry vinegar and 6 tbsp oil. Beat with a fork. Peel the potatoes, cut into thin slices and pour over the egg and herb dressing. Transfer to a serving dish and spoon the cottage cheese into the middle.

CABBAGE AND CHEESE SALAD

Serves 4
½ Savoy cabbage
½ red cabbage
200 g/7 oz hard cheese (e.g. Cheddar)
vinegar flavoured with shallots
1 shallot
4 anchovy fillets in oil
pinch cumin
tabasco
extra virgin olive oil

Rinse and shred the Savoy and red cabbage. Cut the cheese into very thin flakes using a special cheese slice and mix with the cabbage. Heat 4 tbsp vinegar in a saucepan and add the finely chopped shallot and crushed anchovy fillets. Simmer over low heat until the anchovies break up and the shallot is soft. Add the cumin and a few drops of tabasco. Remove from the heat and very gradually beat in 6 tbsp oil. Pour the warm sauce over the salad and mix carefully before serving.

Cabbage and cheese salad

TUNA, EGG AND MACKEREL SALAD

Serves 4

1 tomato

1 tsp anchovy paste

1 tsp tomato purée

150 ml/5 fl oz/⅔ cup mayonnaise

1 tsp capers

1 clove garlic, crushed

freshly ground black pepper

200 g/7 oz lamb's lettuce

1 head fennel

4 hard-boiled eggs

1 can tuna in oil

1 can mackerel in oil

extra virgin olive oil

juice of 1 lemon

P repare the dressing: peel and seed the tomato, then cut into dice. Mix the anchovy paste and tomato purée into the mayonnaise; add the diced tomato, capers and garlic, mix well and sprinkle with pepper. Rinse and dry the lettuce and fennel and thinly slice the latter. Shell and slice the eggs. Drain and flake the tuna and mackerel, and arrange on individual dishes with the eggs and salad. Sprinkle with a trickle of olive oil and lemon juice and serve the mayonnaise dressing separately.

SPICY TUNA SALAD

Serves 4

1 small lettuce

2 tomatoes

1 green or red pepper

300 g/10 oz canned tuna

1 tsp tapénade (black olive paste)

chilli powder

4 anchovy fillets in oil

salt and freshly ground black pepper

1 tbsp chopped gherkins

vinegar flavoured with coriander and chilli

extra virgin olive oil

oregano

R inse and dry the lettuce and tear into pieces. Rinse the tomatoes and cut into wedges. Hold the pepper over a flame until the skin blisters and can be peeled off. Discard the seeds and dice the pepper. Drain and flake the tuna. Mix the tapénade with 2 pinches chilli powder, the chopped anchovies, a little salt and pepper, then add the gherkins, 3 tbsp vinegar and gradually beat in 7 tbsp oil. Mix all the ingredients together in a large bowl and sprinkle with oregano before serving.

Tuna, egg and mackerel salad

CHEESE SALAD WITH GARLIC CROÛTONS

Serves 4

1 lettuce

400 g/14 oz assorted hard and soft cheeses

4 slices wholemeal bread

1 clove garlic

extra virgin olive oil flavoured with thyme

sherry vinegar

2 tbsp sherry

salt and freshly ground black pepper

Trim and rinse the salad and tear into pieces. Dice all the hard cheese and break up the soft cheese with a fork. Toast the bread, rub the slices with garlic and sprinkle with a trickle of oil. Cut into dice and keep warm in the oven. Mix together in a small bowl 2 tbsp vinegar and 5 tbsp oil. Season with salt and pepper. Heat then flame the sherry and add to the vinaigrette. Mix together the salad, cheeses and croûtons and dress with the vinaigrette.

TWO-BEAN SALAD

Serves 4

300 g/10 oz tomatoes

extra virgin olive oil flavoured with bay leaf

sherry vinegar

1 tbsp lemon juice

1 tsp mustard

salt and freshly ground black pepper

400 g/14 oz frozen runner beans

1 can French beans

Blanch the tomatoes in boiling water for 1 minute. Peel them, then place in a food processor with 6 tbsp oil, 2 tbsp vinegar, 1 tbsp lemon juice, the mustard, salt and pepper. Blend to make a sauce, then place in the refrigerator. Meanwhile cook the runner beans according to the manufacturer's instructions, then drain and cut into pieces. Drain the French beans, rinse, dry and add to the runner beans. Dress with a few tbsp tomato sauce and serve the rest separately.

SWEET AND SOUR FRANKFURTER SALAD

Serves 4

4 large frankfurters

4 large gherkins

1 leek

½ tsp fennel seeds

few coriander seeds

1 clove garlic

1 tsp soft brown sugar

cider vinegar

extra virgin olive oil

salt and freshly ground black pepper

1 crisp lettuce

Peel the frankfurters and slice thinly. Thinly slice the gherkins and leek and mix these ingredients together. Using a pestle and mortar grind together the fennel and coriander seeds, the peeled garlic and sugar. Add 3 tbsp vinegar, 6 tbsp oil, salt and pepper and pour over the frankfurters and vegetables. Transfer to a very hot oven for a few minutes before serving on a bed of finely sliced or shredded lettuce.

CAESAR SALAD

Serves 4

1 crisp lettuce

2 hard-boiled eggs

150 g/5 oz/1¼ cups grated Gruyère

4 anchovy fillets, chopped

1 clove garlic, crushed

2 tsp lemon juice

1 egg yolk

salt and freshly ground black pepper

extra virgin olive oil

3 slices wholemeal bread, diced

Trim and rinse the lettuce and tear into pieces. Cut the eggs into quarters and place in a large bowl with the lettuce and cheese. Mix together in a small bowl the anchovies, garlic, lemon juice, egg yolk, plenty of pepper and 4 tbsp oil. Fry the diced bread in olive oil until golden brown, then add to the salad. Pour over the anchovy sauce and mix thoroughly before serving.

BAGNA CAUDA

Serves 4

6 cloves garlic

125 g/4 oz salted anchovies

50 g/2 oz/¼ cup butter

250 ml/9 fl oz/1⅛ cups walnut oil

1 kg/2¼ lb mixed vegetables (peppers, carrots, celery, radicchio, chicory (Belgian endive))

freshly ground black pepper

This delicious garlic and anchovy dip, a traditional speciality of the Piedmont region in northern Italy, is served hot, with crudités. Peel and finely slice the garlic. Rinse the anchovies to remove the salt; dry on kitchen paper and chop coarsely. Melt the butter with the garlic in a flameproof earthenware casserole until the garlic becomes transparent. Gradually add the anchovies and oil. Simmer for 20 minutes, stirring occasionally with a wooden spoon. Meanwhile prepare the vegetables: rinse and trim as usual and cut the peppers into strips, the carrots and celery into matchsticks and the salad into wedges, without removing the central core. When the bagna cauda is ready add pepper to taste and serve very hot, in the center of the table, surrounded by the raw vegetables.

MEXICAN SALAD

Serves 4

300 g/10 oz mixed frozen vegetables, ready diced (peppers, beans, peas etc.)

125 g/4 oz/1 cup frozen sweetcorn

125 g/4 oz frozen carrots

300 g/10 oz/1¼ cups peeled prawns (shrimp)

lemon juice

extra virgin olive oil

fresh or dried mint

1 clove garlic, chopped

Mexican salad

| salt and freshly ground allspice |
| 200 ml/7 fl oz/scant 1 cup mayonnaise |
| 100 ml/3½ fl oz/½ cup single (light) cream |
| 1 frisée lettuce |

Cook the mixed frozen vegetables, sweetcorn and carrots in boiling salted water according to the manufacturer's instructions. Drain and leave to cool. Mix with the prawns (shrimp) in a large bowl. Pour over a dressing made with 2 tbsp lemon juice, 4 tbsp oil, 1 tbsp chopped fresh mint (or 1 tsp dried), the chopped garlic, salt and pepper. In a separate small bowl mix the mayonnaise with 1 tbsp lemon juice, the cream and mint according to taste. Serve the salad on a bed of frisée lettuce and serve the mint-flavoured mayonnaise separately.

ROMANTIC SALADS

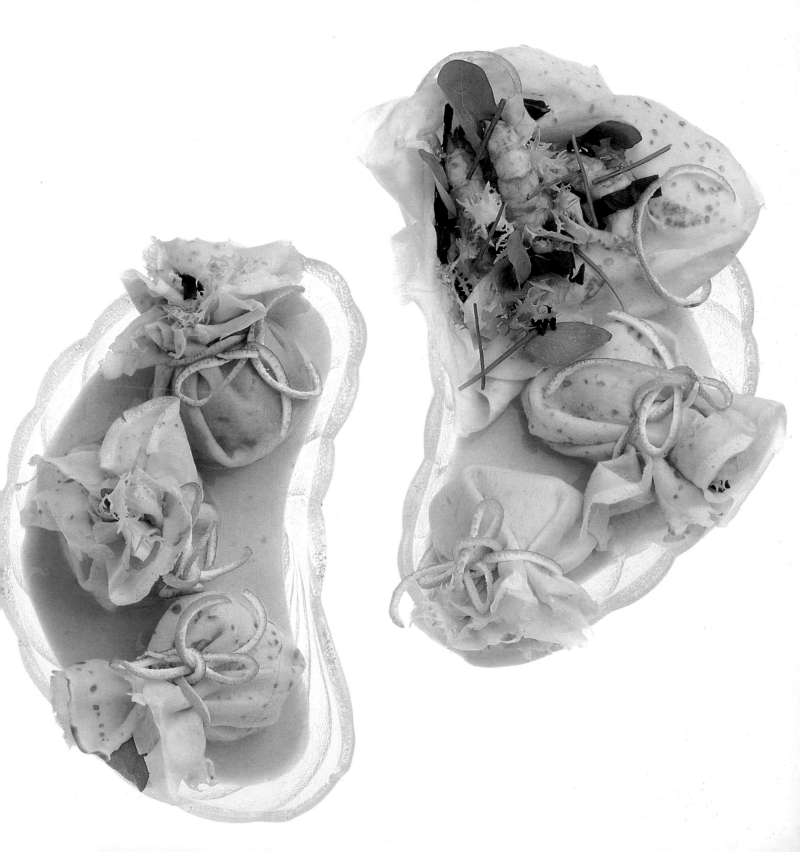

It's the first time you've invited your loved one for supper, or maybe the hundredth and you're feeling uninspired. For your first anniversary you may want to make a special dish, using warm colours and delicately flavoured ingredients, prepared with loving care and attention to detail. Why not create something sweetly romantic and completely different for a St Valentine's Day surprise? These salads can be made subtle or spicy to suit your mood; garnished with flowers and with the delicate fragrance of rose petals, they should be served by candlelight as a tender introduction to a truly romantic evening.

On the previous page:
Crêpes filled with scampi salad

CRÊPES FILLED WITH SCAMPI SALAD

Serves 2

For the crêpes:

125 g/4 oz/1 cup plain (all purpose) flour

2 eggs

100 ml/3½ fl oz/scant ½ cup milk

oil, salt, sugar, butter

For the filling:

125 g/4 oz mixed frisée, lamb's lettuce and radicchio

few chives

12 Dublin Bay prawns (scampi)

butter

1 shallot, chopped

salt and pink pepper

100 ml/3½ fl oz/½ cup single (light) cream

1 tsp lemon juice

3 tbsp dry white wine

Beat together the flour and eggs, gradually adding the milk, 1 tbsp oil and a pinch of salt and sugar. Leave to stand for 30 minutes. Melt ½ tsp butter in a non-stick frying pan, pour in 2 tbsp crêpe batter and tilt the pan to distribute evenly. Cook briefly over high heat on both sides, then slide on to a plate. Make another 3 crêpes in the same way. Rinse the salad and break up the larger leaves. Peel the prawns (scampi), reserving the shells. Use a pestle and mortar to grind the shells with 40 g/1½ oz/3 tbsp butter. Melt this paste in a small saucepan, add the shallot and sauté for 5 minutes. Season with salt and pepper and stir in the cream. When the sauce begins to thicken stir in the lemon juice and white wine. Remove from the heat, strain through a sieve and keep warm. Place a little salad and 3 prawns (scampi) in the middle of each crêpe, enclose the contents and tie into a parcel with a thin strip of lime peel (see illustration on page 43). Place in a hot oven for 1 minute before serving with the warm sauce.

Smoked salmon and cucumber salad

SMOKED SALMON AND CUCUMBER SALAD

Serves 2

1 cucumber

salt and white pepper

1 heart frisée lettuce

6 slices smoked salmon

1 bunch dill

1 tsp soft brown sugar

juice of 1 lime

extra virgin olive oil flavoured with dill

Peel and slice the cucumber, sprinkle lightly with salt and leave to stand for 30 minutes on a clean tea towel. Rinse the lettuce, tear into pieces and mix with the rinsed and dried cucumber slices. Cut two slices of salmon into small squares and mix with the salad. Curl each remaining slice into a rose shape (see illustration on page 45). Place the sugar, lime juice, a large pinch of white pepper, salt and 4 tbsp oil in a small jar and shake until the sugar has dissolved. Dress the salad, place in individual dishes and garnish with the salmon "roses" and freshly chopped dill.

CELERIAC SALAD

Serves 2

250 g/9 oz celeriac

lemon juice

1 egg yolk

1 tsp Dijon mustard

salt and freshly ground black pepper

150 ml/5 fl oz/⅔ cup extra virgin olive oil

2 tbsp single (light) cream

2 hard-boiled eggs

1 carton mustard and cress

Peel the celeriac and cut into matchsticks. Plunge immediately into boiling water acidulated with lemon juice to prevent discoloration; drain after a few seconds and refresh under cold running water. Mix together in a small bowl the egg yolk, mustard and a pinch of salt. Gradually add the oil drop by drop, then, as the mixture emulsifies, in a thin trickle, beating constantly until the mayonnaise is thick and smooth. Incorporate the cream and 1 tbsp lemon juice and adjust the seasoning. Mix 1 tbsp mayonnaise with the celeriac and place in the refrigerator. Slice the eggs and use to garnish the edge of two individual plates. Alternate the slices with bunches of mustard and cress and spoon the celeriac into the center.

Rose petal salad

ROSE PETAL SALAD

Serves 2

3 heads chicory (Belgian endive)

1 small pomegranate

1 rose

freshly ground white and pink pepper

salt

white wine vinegar

extra virgin olive oil

Cut off the base of the chicory (Belgian endive), then rinse and dry the leaves. Arrange on individual plates and sprinkle each with 1–2 tbsp pomegranate seeds and a few rose petals. Sprinkle with a little mixed white and pink pepper. Place the remaining pomegranate seeds in a piece of muslin or cheesecloth and squeeze to extract the juice. Season with salt and pepper, add 2 tbsp vinegar, 4 tbsp oil and beat to obtain a vinaigrette. Pour over the salad just before serving.

FOUR-CHEESE SALAD WITH FENNEL

Serves 2

1 heart frisée lettuce

1 head fennel

50 g/2 oz Parmesan, flaked

50 g/2 oz mild Provolone or similar smoked cheese

50 g/2 oz Camembert

50 g/2 oz goat's cheese

1 tsp fennel seeds

2 slices onion

2 gherkins, chopped

red wine vinegar

extra virgin olive oil

salt and freshly ground black pepper

Vary the cheeses in this recipe according to taste and availability, but try to maintain a balance between hard and soft, strong and mild. Rinse the lettuce and tear into pieces; rinse and finely slice the fennel. Dice all the cheese and add to the salad. Using a mortar and pestle or blender pound the fennel seeds, onion and gherkins to a paste. Gradually beat in 2 tbsp vinegar, 4 tbsp oil and salt and pepper to taste. Dress the salad with the vinaigrette just before serving.

WARM SWEETBREAD SALAD

Serves 2

200 g/7 oz sweetbreads

50 g/2 oz frisée lettuce

Sweetcorn and radish salad with spicy pink dressing

48

50 g/2 oz wild rocket or watercress

1 head radicchio

red wine vinegar

walnut oil

salt and freshly ground black pepper

butter

Soak the sweetbreads for 1 hour, then rinse under running water. Cook for 7–10 minutes in boiling acidulated water, then drain and remove the thin skin. Trim and rinse the lettuces and break up the larger leaves. Make a vinaigrette with 2 tbsp vinegar, 4 tbsp walnut oil, salt and pepper. Divide the dressed salad between two plates. Cut the sweetbreads into walnut-sized pieces and sauté briefly in a frying pan in 2 tbsp melted butter. Sprinkle with salt and pepper and add to the salad after sautéeing for 2 minutes. Serve at once.

SWEETCORN AND RADISH SALAD WITH SPICY PINK DRESSING

Serves 2

80 g/3 oz batavia or lamb's lettuce

6 radishes

½ small white cabbage

6 baby sweetcorn

50 g/2 oz Philadelphia cheese

100 ml/3½ fl oz/½ cup single (light) cream

3 tsp tomato ketchup

lemon juice

1 tbsp paprika

Worcestershire sauce

tabasco

salt and freshly ground black pepper

Rinse and dry the lettuce; trim and thinly slice the radishes. Shred the white cabbage and cut the sweetcorn into rings. Mix these ingredients together and distribute between two plates. Mash the cheese with a fork in a small bowl and stir in the cream and ketchup. Add 1 tbsp lemon juice, the paprika, and a few drops Worcestershire sauce and tabasco according to taste. Adjust the seasoning and serve the dressing separately with the salad.

WARM BEEF AND GREEN PEPPERCORN SALAD

Serves 2

200 g/7 oz beef fillet

1 tbsp green peppercorns in brine

extra virgin olive oil

1 lettuce heart

150 g/5 oz French beans

2 hard-boiled egg yolks

white wine vinegar flavoured with green peppercorns

100 ml/3½ fl oz/½ cup single (light) cream

1 tbsp chopped parsley

1 tbsp chopped onion

salt and freshly ground black pepper

Dice the beef and marinate for at least 1 hour in half the green peppercorns crushed with 2 tbsp oil. Rinse and dry the lettuce and place whole leaves in the bottom of two dishes. String and top the beans and cook for 10 minutes in boiling salted water. Meanwhile sieve the egg yolks and mix with 2 tbsp vinegar and 1 tbsp oil. Gradually stir in the cream and when the sauce is well blended add the remaining green peppercorns, the chopped parsley and onion and a sprinkling of black pepper. Place the marinated beef in a baking pan under a very hot grill until brown on

both sides but still tender. Arrange on the bed of
lettuce with the beans and serve the sauce
separately.

ORANGE, GINGER AND CARROT SALAD

Serves 2

300 g/10 oz carrots

2 small oranges

1 small piece root ginger

strawberry vinegar

salt and freshly ground black pepper

1 tbsp orange juice

extra virgin olive oil

50 g/2 oz crisp lettuce (e.g. batavia)

1 tbsp poppy seeds

Trim and scrape the
carrots, and cut into matchsticks. Steam them
for 10 minutes, then leave to cool. Remove the
peel and all the pith from the oranges and slice
thinly. Peel and finely chop or grate the ginger.
Heat 3 tbsp vinegar and reduce to 1½ tbsp; add
a pinch of salt and pepper, the orange juice and
4 tbsp oil. Pour this dressing over the carrots,
add the ginger and mix well. Chill in the
refrigerator for 2 hours. Before serving add the
rinsed and dried lettuce, arrange on a plate
bordered with the oranges and sprinkle lightly
with poppy seeds.

POTATO SALAD WITH SCAMPI AND CHAMPAGNE

Serves 2

300 g/10 oz new potatoes

salt and freshly ground black pepper

200 g/7 oz cooked Dublin Bay prawn (scampi) tails

champagne or sparkling dry white wine

champagne vinegar

fresh herbs (chives, parsley, basil, dill, thyme, tarragon)

extra virgin olive oil

1 tbsp flaked almonds

Scrub the potatoes under running water to remove any earth. Cook for 15–20 minutes or until tender in boiling salted water; drain and leave to cool. Slice the potatoes without peeling them and place in a salad bowl. Add the Dublin Bay prawns (scampi) tails to the potatoes. Season with salt and pepper and sprinkle with 3–4 tbsp champagne and 2 tbsp champagne vinegar. Add the trimmed and finely chopped herbs and leave to stand in a cool place for a few hours. Before serving sprinkle with a little olive oil, the flaked almonds and more champagne if desired.

WARM FENNEL AND SOLE SALAD WITH MALTESE SAUCE

Serves 2

2 heads fennel

1 head frisée lettuce

2 fillets of sole

paprika

salt and freshly ground black pepper

2 egg yolks

3 tbsp orange juice

125 g/4 oz/½ cup butter

grated rind of 1 orange

1 tsp lemon juice

Trim the fennel and cut into wedges; rinse and dry the lettuce. Sprinkle the fish with a pinch of paprika and pepper and cut each fillet in half. Steam the fennel for 15 minutes, adding the fish to the steamer for the

Orange, ginger and carrot salad

last 5 minutes. Beat the egg yolks and orange juice in a double saucepan or bain-marie and gradually whisk in the melted butter. Remove from the heat, adjust the seasoning and stir in the orange rind, lemon juice and a pinch of paprika. Garnish two plates with a circle of lettuce, place the steamed fennel and fish in the center and cover with the warm sauce.

CELERY SALAD WITH WALNUT DRESSING

Serves 2

1 bunch watercress

1 head green celery

125 ml/4 fl oz/½ cup natural yoghurt

1 tbsp lemon juice

extra virgin olive oil

salt and freshly ground black pepper

2 tbsp chopped walnuts

Rinse the watercress, dry carefully and remove the stalks. Arrange on two plates. Rinse the celery and chop. Mix together the yoghurt, lemon juice, 2 tbsp olive oil, salt and pepper and the walnuts. Mix the celery with 2 tbsp walnut dressing and spoon into the center of each plate. Serve the remaining dressing separately.

CHICKEN SALAD WITH SWEET AND SOUR DRESSING

Serves 2

50 g/2 oz lamb's lettuce

1 lettuce heart

250 g/9 oz cooked chicken

125 g/4 oz fresh pineapple

1 tbsp soft brown sugar

1 tbsp vinegar

garlic salt

Cayenne pepper

freshly ground black pepper

Rinse and dry the lettuce and arrange in two dishes. Cut the chicken into strips and place on the bed of lettuce. Finely chop the pineapple and collect the juice. Heat with the sugar in a small saucepan and when the sugar has dissolved add the vinegar, chopped pineapple, a pinch of garlic salt, Cayenne pepper and black pepper. Stir and leave to cool slightly before pouring over the salad.

QUAIL'S EGG AND PISTACHIO NUT SALAD

Serves 2

150 g/5 oz red oak leaf lettuce (*feuille de chêne*)

1 tomato

10 quails' eggs

1 tbsp shelled pistachio nuts

vinegar flavoured with green peppercorns

extra virgin olive oil

1 bunch chervil

1 tbsp green peppercorns

salt

Rinse and dry the lettuce and slice the tomato. Place the quails' eggs in a saucepan of water and bring to the boil. Remove from the heat immediately and run under cold water. When cool, remove the shells and cut the eggs in half. Blanch the pistachio nuts in boiling water for 1 minute. Drain and peel. Mix 1½ tbsp vinegar with 3 tbsp oil; add 1 tbsp chopped chervil, the chopped green peppercorns and salt to taste. Arrange the lettuce, tomato and eggs in two individual dishes, sprinkle with the vinaigrette and chopped pistachio nuts and garnish with a few sprigs of chervil.

Quail's egg and pistachio nut salad

VEGETARIAN SALADS

Vegetarian diets – of greater or lesser degrees of strictness – are becoming increasingly popular in all kinds of circles, appealing to all age groups. A book devoted entirely to salads is undoubtedly the most suitable vehicle for promoting vegetarian food which, although traditional in many Far Eastern countries, is still relatively new in the West. Being a vegetarian does not mean restricting yourself to fruit and vegetables alone; in order to achieve a well balanced diet you must also include certain other proteins that are not found in fresh vegetables. Cereals and pulses are the most substantial and protein-rich meat substitutes. This chapter illustrates the exciting salads you can make using beans, chickpeas, burghul (cracked wheat), brown rice, barley, lentils and tofu (soya bean "cheese"). All ingredients of ancient origin in the traditional cuisine of certain Eastern countries, they are now enjoying renewed popularity, combined with an infinite variety of accompaniments to tempt even the most resolute carnivore.

On the previous page:
Cracked wheat and seaweed salad

CRACKED WHEAT AND SEAWEED SALAD

Serves 4

125 g/4 oz/⅔ cup cracked wheat

100 g/3½ oz/½ cup chickpeas, soaked overnight

25 g/1 oz dried seaweed

extra virgin olive oil

salt and freshly ground black pepper

soy sauce

Rinse the cracked wheat under cold running water in a sieve, then cook in boiling water for 30 minutes. Drain. Cook the chick peas for 3 hours in unsalted water, then drain. Soak the seaweed for 5 minutes; drain, then cut into strips and cook for 5 minutes in boiling water. Heat 3 tbsp oil in a large frying pan and sauté the chick peas and drained seaweed for a few minutes. Mix with the cracked wheat, season with salt, pepper and soy sauce and serve warm or chilled.

SPRING SALAD

Serves 4

200 g/7 oz/scant 1 cup pearl barley

salt and freshly ground allspice

1 carrot

1 head radicchio

few leaves frisée lettuce

few leaves escarole

black and green olives

few sprigs fennel

50 g/2 oz soybean sprouts

½ clove garlic

juice of 1 lemon

extra virgin olive oil

Spring salad

Rinse the pearl barley thoroughly to remove excess starch. Bring a large saucepan of water to the boil and cook the pearl barley for 1½ hours. Drain and rinse under cold water. Meanwhile prepare the vegetables: peel and grate the carrot and tear the lettuce into pieces; pit a few olives and chop coarsely with the fennel. Place all these ingredients in a large bowl with the pearl barley and soybean sprouts and add a few whole olives and the crushed garlic. Make a dressing with the lemon juice, 6 tbsp oil and plenty of salt and pepper. Pour over the salad and chill or leave to stand for 30 minutes before serving.

SPINACH SALAD WITH RICE FLAKES

Serves 4

2 tsp mustard

juice of 1 lemon

3 tbsp natural yoghurt

salt and freshly ground black pepper

125 ml/4 fl oz/½ cup extra virgin olive oil

5 radishes

3 tbsp rice flakes

3 tbsp rolled oats

1 courgette (zucchini)

1 carrot

1 kg/2¼ lb spinach

Mix together in a small bowl the mustard, lemon juice and yoghurt. Season with salt and pepper and gradually beat in the oil before adding the trimmed and chopped radishes. Soak the rice flakes and oats for 5 minutes in boiling water, then drain, mix with 2 tbsp dressing and leave to stand for 20 minutes. Trim the courgette (zucchini) and carrot and cut both into slices, then into matchsticks. Shred the spinach finely. Distribute the vegetables and cereals between individual plates and sprinkle with a little dressing. Serve the rest separately.

RICE AND MUSHROOM SALAD

Serves 4

450 g/1 lb button mushrooms

salt and freshly ground black pepper

extra virgin olive oil

1 bay leaf

2 tbsp chopped onion

1 tbsp soft brown sugar

1 tsp freshly ground coriander

pinch ground cinnamon

pinch Cayenne pepper

pinch freshly ground allspice

4 tbsp red wine vinegar

200 g/7 oz/generous 1 cup parboiled brown rice

Clean and slice the mushrooms, then cook for 2 minutes in boiling salted water. Drain. Heat 6 tbsp oil and the bay leaf in a frying pan. Add the onion and fry gently with the sugar and spices for 1 minute. Add the mushrooms and vinegar and fry gently for 5 minutes. Remove from the heat and leave to cool. Cook the brown rice for 30 minutes or until tender in boiling salted water. Drain and mix with the mushrooms and their juice. Season with plenty of black pepper, stir well and add more oil if necessary. Chill for 2 hours before serving.

SOYBEAN SALAD

Serves 4

250 g/9 oz/1⅓ cups soybeans

3 tomatoes

Spinach salad with rice flakes

salt and freshly ground black pepper

white wine vinegar

extra virgin olive oil

1 large bunch mixed fresh herbs (e.g. chervil, mint, tarragon, parsley, chives, marjoram)

2 cloves garlic

Soak the soybeans overnight, then drain and cook in unsalted boiling water for 1½–2 hours or until tender. Drain and leave to cool. Meanwhile plunge the tomatoes into boiling water for 1 minute. Drain and peel, then remove the seeds and chop coarsely. Season with salt and pepper and sprinkle with 3 tbsp vinegar and 8 tbsp oil. Add the freshly chopped herbs and the peeled but whole garlic cloves and leave to stand while the soybeans are cooking. Mix the cold cooked soybeans with the tomatoes and herbs and stir well before serving.

BEAN, LEEK AND HERB SALAD

Serves 4

200 g/7 oz/⅔ cup borlotti or lima beans, soaked overnight

2 bay leaves

few sprigs rosemary

1 leek

1 bunch basil

vinegar flavoured with garlic

extra virgin olive oil

salt and freshly ground black pepper

Drain the beans; place in a saucepan, cover with water, and add the bay leaves and 2 sprigs rosemary. Bring to the boil and simmer gently for 1½ hours. Meanwhile trim and rinse the leek; cut into thin rings and soak in cold water for 1 hour, changing the water occasionally. Trim and cut up the basil and

chop 1 sprig rosemary. Drain the beans when tender and, while still hot, mix them with the herbs, drained leek, 3 tbsp vinegar and 6 tbsp oil. Sprinkle with salt and plenty of freshly ground pepper and serve either warm or cold.

RICE AND LENTIL SALAD

Serves 4

125 g/4 oz/⅔ cup patna (long-grain) rice

2 tbsp wild rice

vegetable stock

150 g/5 oz/½ cup cooked brown lentils

1 tomato

1 cooked carrot

1 bunch fresh basil

parsley

chives

1 clove garlic

salt and freshly ground black pepper

cider vinegar

extra virgin olive oil

1 frisée lettuce

Cook both types of rice together in 450 ml/16 fl oz/2 cups vegetable stock in a covered saucepan until the rice has completely absorbed the liquid. Turn the cooked rice on to a clean cloth, separate the grains with a fork and leave to cool. Mix the lentils with the diced tomato and carrot. Trim and finely chop the herbs and add together with ½ clove crushed garlic to the rice. Season with salt and pepper, 2 tbsp vinegar and olive oil. Rinse and dry the lettuce and tear into pieces; mix half with the rice and place the rest on a serving dish. Cover with the rice and lentil salad and serve.

Bean, leek and herb salad

BREAD SALAD

Serves 4

250 g/9 oz stale bread, unsliced

2 large tomatoes

1 small onion

½ cucumber

1 bunch fresh basil

salt and freshly ground black pepper

red wine vinegar

extra virgin olive oil

Cut the bread into cubes, place in a bowl of water and leave to stand for a few minutes. Squeeze out excess water and transfer to a clean bowl. Add the finely sliced tomatoes and onion, the peeled and sliced cucumber and the roughly torn up basil leaves. Season with salt and pepper and leave to stand for 2–3 hours. Just before serving, dress the salad with 4 tbsp red wine vinegar and plenty of olive oil. Stir carefully and add a few fresh basil leaves.

COUSCOUS SALAD

Serves 4

turmeric

extra virgin olive oil

250 g/9 oz precooked couscous

¼ yellow pepper

¼ red pepper

1 small aubergine (eggplant)

1 courgette (zucchini)

2 cloves garlic, unpeeled

1 tsp cumin seeds

salt and freshly ground black pepper

chilli powder or paprika

Bring 300 ml/10 fl oz/ 1¼ cups salted water to the boil; add the turmeric and 1 tbsp oil, then the couscous. Remove from the heat, cover and leave to stand for 5 minutes. Turn the couscous out on to a tray and separate the grains with a fork. Trim and rinse all the vegetables and cut into dice. Heat 4 tbsp oil in a frying pan and add the garlic and cumin seeds. Add the diced vegetables and sauté for 10 minutes, seasoning with salt and pepper. Mix the couscous and vegetables together in a large bowl and stir well. Sprinkle with chilli powder or paprika.

―――

TABBOULEH

Serves 4

200 g/7 oz/generous 1 cup cracked wheat

1 bunch parsley

4 spring onions (scallions)

1 bunch mint

4 tomatoes

salt and freshly ground black pepper

4 tbsp lemon juice

extra virgin olive oil

Soak the cracked wheat for 20 minutes in cold water. Drain and press out all excess water. Finely chop the parsley, discarding the stalks. Finely chop the spring onion (scallion), including the green part. Finely chop the mint. Place the cracked wheat in a large bowl with the mint, parsley and spring onions (scallions). Add the coarsely chopped tomatoes and season with salt and pepper, the lemon juice and olive oil. Chill in the refrigerator before serving.

―――

Couscous salad

PITTA BREAD WITH EGG SALAD

Serves 4

4 hard-boiled eggs

3 tbsp mayonnaise

4 tbsp natural yoghurt

2 tbsp roasted peanuts

1 spring onion (scallion)

1 bunch watercress

salt and freshly ground black pepper

4 pitta bread

1 lettuce heart

Peel the eggs and mash to a paste with the mayonnaise and yoghurt. Add the chopped peanuts and finely sliced spring onion (scallion) and the trimmed, rinsed and coarsely chopped watercress, then season with salt and pepper. Fill the pocket of each pitta bread with a few rinsed lettuce leaves and a quarter of the egg mixture. The pitta bread can be heated before being filled if preferred.

WATERCRESS, TOFU AND KUMQUAT SALAD

Serves 4

1 large bunch watercress

10 kumquats

250 g/9 oz tofu

1 tbsp sesame seeds

1 tbsp tahini (sesame paste)

2 tbsp rice vinegar

2 tbsp sherry

1 tbsp soy sauce

1 clove garlic, chopped

4 tbsp sesame or soybean oil

salt

Rinse and dry the watercress. Rinse, dry and finely slice the kumquats. Cut the tofu into large dice. Distribute these ingredients between four plates and sprinkle with sesame seeds. In a small bowl mix together the tahini, vinegar, sherry, soy sauce, garlic and oil. Taste the dressing before adding salt. For a less spicy dressing, use only tahini, oil and vinegar.

WILD RICE SALAD

Serves 4

125 g/4 oz/⅔ cup wild rice

salt and freshly ground black pepper

600 g/1¼ lb endive (chicory)

50 g/2 oz/¼ cup butter

3 tbsp lemon juice

Soak the wild rice in cold water for 1 hour. Drain and cook, covered, in 150 ml/9 fl oz/1⅛ cups boiling salted water for 40–45 minutes or until all the liquid has been absorbed. Turn the rice out on to a baking tray and keep warm. Rinse the endive (chicory). Cook briefly in boiling water, then drain, shred, and add to the rice. Melt the butter in a small saucepan. When it begins to foam add the lemon juice, salt and pepper. Pour over the wild rice salad and serve at once.

Watercress, tofu and kumquat salad

COUNTRY SALADS

Here are some salad recipes using ingredients which may be the fruits of your leisure time, either grown or caught in the pursuit of your favourite pastime. Perhaps fishing is your sport and you set off every weekend, armed with rod and bait in search of an obliging trout. Or you may prefer shooting and need new ideas on how to present your game. Maybe you are a keen gardener with a vegetable plot and flower beds a riot of colour in spring. Whatever your preference, virtually any harvest can be served at table. Just as primitive man survived simply by eating what he could catch or cultivate, so you can amuse yourselves by inviting friends to join you in a truly home-grown supper.

On the previous page:
Garden salad

Duck breast salad with Madeira dressing

GARDEN SALAD

Serves 4

1 head red lettuce

200 g/7 oz mixed lettuce, freshly picked

8 young courgettes (zucchini)

1 tomato

1 carrot

125 g/4 oz mange tout (snow peas)

6 Brussels sprouts

salt and freshly ground black pepper

8 marrow (squash) flowers

2 sticks celery

1 tbsp coarse grain mustard

sherry vinegar

extra virgin olive oil

Rinse the lettuce, courgettes (zucchini); peel and slice the carrot and tomato. Trim the mange tout (snow peas) and remove the outer leaves from the Brussels sprouts. Bring a saucepan of lightly salted water to the boil and cook the mange tout (snow peas) for 1 minute, and the carrot and Brussels sprouts for 10 minutes. Tear the lettuce leaves into pieces and arrange on a serving dish. Place the vegetables on top: the whole courgettes (zucchini); the sprouts, cut in half; the tomato, cut into wedges; the mange tout (snow peas); carrots; and the marrow (squash) flowers, cut in half. Rinse and finely chop the celery and mix with the mustard, 3 tbsp sherry vinegar, 7 tbsp oil, salt and pepper to make a dressing. Pour the dressing over the salad just before serving.

DUCK BREAST SALAD WITH MADEIRA DRESSING

Serves 4

2 heads red Treviso chicory or radicchio

1 bunch Catalonia chicory or lamb's lettuce

---

2 duck breasts

3 juniper berries

salt and freshly ground black pepper

butter

2 tbsp red wine vinegar

6 tbsp Madeira

Trim and rinse the red chicory and separate the leaves. Separate the tops from the Catalonia chicory and use only the most tender leaves. Soak them in cold water for 1 hour, then drain and dry. Arrange both types of chicory on a large serving dish. Cut the duck breast in half and rub in the crushed juniper berries, a little salt and plenty of pepper. Melt 4 tbsp butter in a frying pan and brown the duck on both sides. Pour off the fat and add 2 tbsp fresh butter. Pour over the vinegar and Madeira and cook for 5–10 minutes, depending on the thickness of the meat. The skin should be golden brown and crisp and the inside slightly pink. Adjust the seasoning and remove from the heat. Leave to stand for 1 minute, then slice and arrange on the bed of lettuce with the slices overlapping. Pour over the strained cooking juices and serve warm.

▬

SORREL AND SWEET VIOLET SALAD

Serves 4

1 small green lettuce

1 small frisée lettuce

few sweet violet leaves

1 bunch freshly picked sweet violets

10 sorrel leaves

mulberry vinegar

extra virgin olive oil

salt and freshly ground black pepper

Trim and rinse the lettuce and tear into pieces. Distribute between individual plates and add the violet leaves and flowers, and the thinly sliced sorrel. Make a dressing by beating together 3 tbsp mulberry vinegar, a large pinch salt and 6 tbsp oil. Pour the dressing over the salad, sprinkle generously with black pepper and serve immediately.

▬

BROAD BEAN AND SUMMER SAVORY SALAD

Serves 4

2 kg/4½ lb broad beans

salt and freshly ground black pepper

1 bunch summer savory

2 spring onions (scallions)

extra virgin olive oil

Shell the beans and, unless they are very tender, remove the outer skin from each bean. Cook for 5–10 minutes in boiling lightly salted water with half the summer savory. Drain when tender and mix with the chopped spring onions (scallions), 1 tbsp chopped summer savory, plenty of oil and black pepper. Serve warm or cold.

▬

WHITE SALAD WITH BLUE CHEESE DRESSING

Serves 4

1 small cauliflower

200 g/7 oz Gruyère

1 heart escarole

50 g/2 oz soft Gorgonzola or Roquefort

125 ml/4 fl oz/½ cup natural yoghurt

Sorrel and sweet violet salad

125 ml/4 fl oz/½ cup mayonnaise

1 shallot

salt and freshly ground black pepper

Divide the cauliflower into florets; rinse, dry and slice thinly. Dice the Gruyère. Rinse and dry the escarole and tear into pieces. Mash the blue cheese with a fork and mix in the yoghurt until smooth. Stir in the mayonnaise and chopped shallot and season with salt and pepper if necessary. Mix the salad ingredients together in a large bowl and serve the blue cheese dressing separately.

SMOKED TROUT SALAD WITH LIME AND DILL

Serves 4

2 small smoked trout

200 g/7 oz lamb's lettuce or escarole

1 head fennel

1 lime

1 bunch dill

salt and freshly ground black pepper

2 tbsp mayonnaise

150 ml/5 fl oz/⅔ cup sour cream

Cut off and discard the head and tail of the trout; remove the skin and bones to leave 4 whole fillets. Trim and rinse the salad; rinse the fennel and slice thinly. Arrange the salad and fennel on individual plates, place the trout fillets on top and garnish with thin slices of lime and a few sprigs of dill. Sprinkle with freshly ground black pepper and a few drops of lime juice. Mix together the mayonnaise, sour cream, 2 tbsp chopped dill, salt and pepper. Serve the sour cream sauce separately.

WILD ROCKET SALAD

Serves 4

1 bunch wild rocket

150 g/5 oz mixed lettuce

1 bunch dandelion leaves

8 cherry tomatoes

10 daisies

white wine vinegar

extra virgin olive oil

salt and freshly ground black pepper

Rinse all the salad ingredients which should, ideally, be freshly picked. Place in a salad bowl with the halved tomatoes and freshly picked daisies. Make a dressing with vinegar, oil, salt and black pepper and pour over the salad just before serving.

FLORAL SALAD

Serves 4

1 bunch purslane leaves

1 large bunch (125 g/4 oz) watercress

8 sweet violets

8 nasturtium flowers

1 rose

few chives

1 sprig marjoram

few basil leaves

red wine vinegar

walnut oil

salt and freshly ground black pepper

1 sprig lavender

Pull the leaves off the purslane and watercress and place in a salad bowl with the nasturtiums, violets and a few rose petals. Using kitchen scissors, cut up the

Smoked trout salad with lime and dill

Freshwater crayfish salad

chives, marjoram and basil leaves and sprinkle over the salad. Mix together in a small bowl 2 tbsp vinegar, 6 tbsp oil, salt, pepper and the lavender flowers. Leave to stand for 20 minutes, pour over the salad and serve at once.

FRESHWATER CRAYFISH SALAD

Serves 4

2 carrots

4 sticks celery

6 spring onions (scallions)

1 liter/1¾ pints/4½ cups dry white wine

1 bay leaf

1 clove

6 black peppercorns

salt and freshly ground black pepper

150/5 oz French beans

2 bunches radishes

40 freshwater crayfish

200 ml/7 fl oz/scant 1 cup mayonnaise

2 tbsp single (light) cream

1 tbsp chopped parsley

1 small bunch celery leaves

1 clove garlic

1 lemon

Trim and rinse all the vegetables and cut the carrots and celery into matchsticks. Cut the spring onions (scallions) lengthwise into four. Heat the wine and ½ liter/18 fl oz/2¼ cups water with the bay leaf, clove, peppercorns and a little salt. When it begins to boil add all the vegetables except the radishes and simmer for about 5 minutes or until tender. Drain, reserving the liquid, and arrange the vegetables on individual plates. Wash the crayfish thoroughly and cook in the court bouillon for 5 minutes. Drain, reserving 1 ladle court bouillon, and place 10 crayfish on each

plate. Reduce the court bouillon to 2 tbsp over high heat, then stir into the mayonnaise with the cream, parsley, chopped celery leaves, crushed garlic and 2 tbsp lemon juice. Serve the sauce in individual dishes so that each guest can dip in the vegetables and crayfish.

GREEN SALAD WITH DEEP-FRIED BORAGE

Serves 4

For the salad:

200 g/7 oz lamb's lettuce, escarole, etc.

20 borage leaves

oil for frying

juice of 1 lemon

extra virgin olive oil

salt, pepper and ground nutmeg

1 tbsp freshly picked borage flowers

For the batter:

125 g/4 oz/1 cup plain (all-purpose) flour

salt, oil

2 eggs

200 ml/7 fl oz/scant 1 cup milk or water

Rinse and dry the salad and distribute between individual plates. Wash the borage only if necessary, then dry thoroughly. Make the batter by mixing together in a bowl the flour, a pinch of salt, 2 tbsp oil and 2 egg yolks. Add the milk or water and whisk until smooth. Leave to stand for 1 hour, then fold in 1 stiffly beaten egg white. Heat the oil for frying; dip the borage leaves one at a time in the batter, then fry in the hot oil. Make a vinaigrette with the lemon juice, 4 tbsp olive oil, salt, pepper and nutmeg and pour over the salad. Arrange the fried borage leaves on top and garnish with a few borage flowers.

TOMATO SALAD WITH PINE NUTS

Serves 4

1 bunch basil

1 bunch chives

1 clove garlic

sea salt and freshly ground black pepper

extra virgin olive oil

2 tbsp white wine vinegar

2 tbsp pine nuts

6 large tomatoes

Rinse the herbs, cut the chives into short pieces, then crush in a mortar the garlic and a few grains of sea salt. Gradually stir in 7 tbsp oil with the pestle; when the paste is smooth, sprinkle with pepper and add the vinegar. Toast the pine nuts lightly. Rinse and slice the tomatoes and arrange on a large serving dish. Pour over the herb vinaigrette and sprinkle with toasted pine nuts.

ARTICHOKE, MUSHROOM AND BACON SALAD

Serves 4

1 can artichokes

200 g/7 oz lamb's lettuce, batavia or watercress

8 button mushrooms

salt and freshly ground black pepper

200 g/7 oz streaky bacon

extra virgin olive oil

few sprigs thyme

3 tbsp vinegar

Drain the artichokes and slice very thinly. Trim, rinse and dry the lettuce and mushrooms. Slice the latter, drain the artichokes and arrange on individual plates with the lettuce. Sprinkle with salt and pepper. Dice the bacon and sauté for a few minutes. Pour off the fat, then add 4 tbsp oil and the thyme. When the bacon is crisp and golden, pour in the vinegar and remove from the heat. Pour the bacon and cooking juices over the salad and serve at once.

COURGETTE (ZUCCHINI) SALAD WITH SWEET AND SOUR DRESSING

Serves 4

2 heads radicchio

3 courgettes (zucchini)

extra virgin olive oil

salt

1 bunch fresh mint

1 tbsp dark soft brown sugar

white wine vinegar

Rinse the radicchio and tear the larger leaves into pieces; leave the hearts whole. Trim and finely slice the courgettes (zucchini). Heat plenty of oil in a frying pan and fry the courgettes (zucchini) a few at a time until they begin to brown. Drain on kitchen paper, reserving the cooking oil, and sprinkle with salt. When all the courgettes (zucchini) are cooked, place in a large bowl with the radicchio, cut a handful of mint leaves into pieces with scissors and sprinkle over. Heat the sugar in a small saucepan; as soon as it begins to caramelize stir in 4 tbsp vinegar. Remove from the heat and add a few tbsp of the oil in which the courgettes (zucchini) were cooked. Dress the salad with the sweet and sour vinaigrette and chill in the refrigerator before serving.

Artichoke, mushroom and bacon salad

EXOTIC SALADS

Although the cuisine of the Western world is extremely rich in variety, this does not prevent us from being tempted by the culinary traditions of far-off lands when an occasion calls for something a little different. To lend a meal that extra special quality, we can borrow entire recipes or just a few characteristic ingredients from the exotic repertoire of Eastern gastronomy. Spices are particularly evocative of distant places, calling to mind ancient aromas of sun-drenched lands. Turmeric, cumin, chilli and curry powder seem to reflect the colours of the earth of their native countries; just a pinch will suffice to transport you on a journey through the senses. The selection in this chapter includes both traditional and specially created recipes, all of which will delight and surprise both the cook and the guests.

On the previous page:
Rice salad with tropical fruit

RICE SALAD WITH TROPICAL FRUIT

Serves 4

250 g/9 oz/1½ cups basmati rice

salt and freshly ground pink pepper

1 carambola (star fruit)

1 mango

1 small papaya

4 slices fresh pineapple

50 g/2 oz seedless grapes

50 g/2 oz/½ cup flaked almonds

juice of 2 lemons

walnut oil

ground cloves

Rinse the rice well under cold running water, then cook in boiling salted water, according to the manufacturer's instructions, until tender. Drain and leave to cool. Peel all the fruit and cut into dice or slices. Toast the almonds lightly. Mix together the rice, fruit and toasted almonds. Make a dressing with the lemon juice, 3 tbsp oil, a large pinch of salt, ¼ tsp ground cloves and freshly ground pink pepper. Pour the dressing over the rice salad and chill for at least 1 hour, stirring occasionally, before serving.

TACOS WITH SPICY MEAT SALAD

Serves 4

extra virgin olive oil

1 clove garlic, chopped

1 onion, chopped

225 g/8 oz/1¼ cups ground beef

3 large plum tomatoes (fresh or canned)

pinch sugar

Tacos with spicy
meat salad

2 green chilli peppers

salt and freshly ground black pepper

1 tbsp freshly chopped coriander

few leaves iceberg lettuce

¼ yellow pepper

1 tomato

8 ready-made taco shells

Heat 3 tbsp oil in a frying pan and sauté the garlic and onion. Add the ground beef and when browned, stir in the sieved tomatoes, sugar and the seeded and chopped chillis. Cook over high heat for 10 minutes, adjust the seasoning and sprinkle with coriander. Keep the meat warm while preparing the salad: rinse the lettuce and cut into strips; slice the yellow pepper and tomato. Heat the taco shells in the oven; when crisp fill them with the meat and mixed salad vegetables. Serve at once.

———

EGYPTIAN BEAN AND EGG SALAD

Serves 4

8 hard-boiled eggs

1 kg/2¼ lb broad beans

salt and freshly ground black pepper

1 bunch summer savory

extra virgin olive oil

2 dried red chilli peppers

1 tsp ground cumin

coriander leaves

Shell the beans and cook in boiling salted water with the summer savory for 10 minutes. Drain and peel off the thin outer skin. Mix together in a small bowl 6 tbsp oil, the finely sliced peppers, cumin, salt and a little pepper. Leave to stand for at least 1 hour, then pour the dressing over the beans. Shell the eggs, cut them in half and serve with the beans. Garnish with coriander leaves.

———

WARM ORIENTAL VEGETABLE SALAD

Serves 4

200 g/7 oz/1¼ cups long-grain rice

salt and freshly ground black pepper

6 leaves Chinese leaf

1 courgette (zucchini)

50 g/2 oz Japanese radish (daikon)

125 g/4 oz French beans

2 sticks celery

1 carrot

2 spring onions (scallions)

125 g/4 oz turnip tops

1 clove garlic

1 bunch coriander

2 large tomatoes

extra virgin olive oil

white wine vinegar

soy sauce

Cook the rice for 5 minutes in boiling salted water, then drain and dry. Place the Chinese leaves in the basket of a steamer and cover with the rice. Trim and rinse all the vegetables, cut into small pieces and place on top of the rice with the finely sliced garlic. Place a few coriander leaves in the water in the bottom of the steamer, place the basket on top and steam, covered, for 25–30 minutes. When the rice is almost tender, add the chopped tomatoes and coriander; cover and leave to cool a little before bringing to the table. Sprinkle with salt, pepper, oil, vinegar and soy sauce, and serve warm.

———

Egyptian bean and egg salad

CHINESE STIR-FRIED SALAD

Serves 4

½ red pepper

3 bunches wild chicory

125 g/4 oz lean pork

soybean oil

125 g/4 oz prawns (shrimp)

salt

2 tbsp rice wine vinegar

soy sauce

1 clove garlic, unpeeled

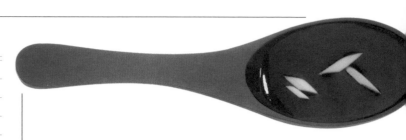

Cut the pepper into fine strips, then dice. Cut the chicory into very thin strips, rinse and dry thoroughly. Chop the meat into dice or thin strips. Heat 3 tbsp soybean oil in a cast iron frying pan or wok and stir-fry the meat for 2 minutes until browned. Add the peppers, stir-fry for 2 minutes, then add the prawns (shrimp). Sprinkle with salt, stir in the vinegar and 1 tbsp soy sauce. Stir well, remove from the heat and keep warm. Deep-fry the chicory in plenty of hot oil to which you have added the unpeeled whole clove of garlic. As soon as the chicory is crisp, remove with a slotted spoon, drain on kitchen paper, then mix with the pork and prawns (shrimp). Serve immediately.

GREEK SALAD

Serves 4

1 small cucumber

salt and freshly ground black pepper

1 green pepper

450 g/1 lb ripe tomatoes

125 g/4 oz/⅔ cup black olives

250 g/9 oz Feta cheese

½ onion, sliced

1 bunch basil

fresh marjoram

extra virgin olive oil

red wine vinegar

Slice the cucumber, sprinkle lightly with salt and leave to stand for 10 minutes. Rinse and seed the pepper, then chop coarsely. Slice the tomatoes, stone the olives and dice the cheese. Arrange layers of tomatoes, pepper, onion, cucumber, olives and cheese on a large serving dish; sprinkle with chopped basil and marjoram, and plenty of black pepper, and dress with oil and vinegar. Serve with slices of crusty bread. Do not add extra salt as the Feta cheese is already very salty.

CHICKEN AND RED PEPPER SALAD WITH CHILLI DRESSING

Serves 4

4 chicken breasts

chicken stock

50 g/2 oz mange tout (snow peas)

1 small red pepper

soybean oil

salt and freshly ground black pepper

2 spring onions (scallions)

4 tbsp sherry vinegar

chilli sauce

Remove any fat and gristle from the chicken breasts and cook for 15–20 minutes in the hot stock. Drain and leave to cool, then cut into strips. Cut the mange tout (snow peas) diagonally into pieces. Trim and seed the pepper; rinse and dry, cut into pieces and sauté in hot oil for 2 minutes with the mange tout (snow peas). Season with salt and pepper.

Cut the spring onions (scallions) into diagonal slices, including the green part, and leave to soak in cold water for ½ hour, changing the water 2 or 3 times. Drain, then mix all the ingredients together in a bowl. Reduce the vinegar over high heat to 1 tbsp; mix with 2 tbsp oil and 2 tbsp chilli sauce, then pour the dressing over the salad. Mix well before serving.

Chicken and red pepper salad with chilli dressing

TARAMASALATA WITH CRUDITÉS

Serves 4

125 g/4 oz/1⅓ cups fresh wholemeal breadcrumbs

juice of 2 lemons

2 cloves garlic

125 g/4 oz/½ cup smoked cod's roe

extra virgin olive oil

4 carrots

2 celery hearts

1 red pepper

wholemeal croûtons

Place the fresh breadcrumbs in a bowl with the lemon juice and 4 tbsp water. Leave to stand for 10 minutes. Transfer to a blender or food processor and add the chopped garlic, cod's roe and 4–5 tbsp olive oil. Blend the mixture until it is smooth, then spoon into individual dishes. Cut the carrots, celery and seeded red pepper into matchsticks. Toast the wholemeal croûtons and place a few with the carrots, celery, red pepper and taramasalata on a plate for each guest.

TURKISH CARROT SALAD

Serves 4

500 g/generous 1 lb carrots

300 g/10 oz potatoes

salt and freshly ground black pepper

80 g/3 oz/½ cup shelled and peeled hazelnuts (filberts)

50 g/2 oz/⅔ cup fresh breadcrumbs

3 cloves garlic

250 ml/9 fl oz/1⅛ cups extra virgin olive oil

5 tbsp white wine vinegar

Trim, rinse and peel the carrots and potatoes. Cook in boiling salted water for 15–20 minutes or until tender, then drain. Meanwhile grind the hazelnuts (filberts) in a blender or food processor; add the breadcrumbs, 1 tbsp water, the chopped garlic and 1 tsp salt. Gradually add the oil and blend until smooth, then add the vinegar and adjust the seasoning. Slice the carrots and potatoes and pour over the cold hazelnut (filbert) dressing.

CURRIED VEGETABLE SALAD

Serves 4

200 g/7 oz mange tout (snow peas)

200 g/7 oz cauliflower

1 small cucumber

salt

200 g/7 oz frozen baby carrots

50 g/2 oz beansprouts

1 onion

butter

curry powder

125 ml/4 fl oz/⅔ cup single (light) cream

150 ml/5 fl oz/⅔ cup natural yoghurt

Cook the mange tout (snow peas) in boiling water for 4–5 minutes. Separate the cauliflower into florets and cook until tender but still crisp. Score the skin of the cucumber lengthwise in strips; slice finely, sprinkle with salt and leave to stand for 20 minutes. Cook the carrots for 5 minutes, drain, then place with all the vegetables, cucumber and beansprouts on a serving dish. Coarsely chop the onion, then sauté in 3 tbsp butter. When it becomes transparent, stir in curry powder to taste and heat for a few minutes before adding the cream. Allow to thicken slightly, then remove from the heat and add the yoghurt. Adjust the seasoning, then pour the warm curried dressing over the vegetables. Adjust the amount of curry powder used to suit your taste.

Curried vegetable salad

ORANGE AND BLACK OLIVE SALAD

Serves 4

4 large oranges

salt and freshly ground black pepper

1 small onion, chopped

125 g/4 oz/⅔ cup black olives, pitted

extra virgin olive oil

few watercress leaves

Peel the oranges, removing all the pith, and slice thinly. Arrange on a serving dish, sprinkle with salt and pepper, then cover with the chopped onion and pitted olives. Pour over a few tbsp olive oil and leave to chill in the refrigerator for ½ hour before serving. Garnish with a few watercress leaves.

■

VEGETABLE SALAD WITH COCONUT DRESSING

Serves 4

1 bunch watercress

125 g/4 oz/1 cup grated carrot

125 g/4 oz Chinese leaf

1 bunch radishes

1 spring onion (scallion)

1 tbsp chopped mint

1 slice shrimp paste (trasi)

vegetable oil

1 clove garlic

salt

Cayenne pepper

sugar

flesh of ½ coconut, grated

juice of ½–1 lemon

Rinse and trim the watercress. Rinse and finely slice all the other vegetables and place in a large bowl with the mint. Fry the shrimp paste for a few minutes, then pound in a mortar with the garlic, a pinch each of salt, Cayenne pepper and sugar. Add the grated coconut, moisten with lemon juice and stir well. Pour the coconut dressing over the salad and mix well before serving.

■

CARROT AND CHINESE LEAF TERRINE

Serves 4

4 large carrots

1 head Chinese leaf

salt and freshly ground black pepper

1 lettuce

soy sauce

1 tbsp grated root ginger

sherry vinegar

Line a loaf tin or rectangular plastic container with foil. Trim and peel the carrots and grate finely. Rinse the Chinese leaf and slice as finely as possible. Place the vegetables in two separate saucepans, sprinkle with salt and pepper, then heat gently until all the water has evaporated. Press out any remaining liquid. Plunge the lettuce into boiling water for a few seconds. Drain, separate the leaves and dry on a clean cloth. Place a layer of lettuce leaves in the bottom of the container, then a layer of carrots on top and another layer of lettuce. Add a layer of Chinese leaf covered with more lettuce, then the remaining carrots with the last lettuce leaves on top. Cover with foil, place a heavy weight on top and chill in the refrigerator for a few hours or overnight. To serve, unmould the terrine and cut into thick slices. Make a dressing by mixing together 3 tbsp soy sauce, the grated ginger and 1 tbsp vinegar.

Carrot and Chinese leaf terrine

pepper. Transfer to a serving dish, garnish with the reserved beetroot and a few whole mint leaves. Chill in the refrigerator for 1 hour before serving.

PERSIAN BEETROOT SALAD

Serves 4

2 small cooked beetroot

200 ml / 7 fl oz / scant 1 cup natural yoghurt

1 tbsp chopped fresh mint

lemon juice

salt and freshly ground black pepper

few mint leaves

Peel and dice the beetroot. Reserve 1 tbsp and mix the rest with the yoghurt, mint, 1 tbsp lemon juice, salt and

HEALTHY SALADS

To be fit and healthy is the principal objective of our times. The recipes included in this section are not geared to specific diets, but rather made up of ingredients with high nutritional and therapeutic value. Everyone knows the properties of oranges, rich in vitamin C, of spinach, which is rich in iron, and of bran as a cleanser of the system. There are few natural products that do not possess particular characteristics beneficial to our health. A good diet that takes into account this aspect may not actually provide a cure, but could be a preventive aid and keep us in good shape. This means keeping fit becomes more than something just fashionable: it is taking care of the body and looking after it in the purest, simplest and most enjoyable way: through eating well.

On the previous page:
Carrot salad with yoghurt
and redcurrants

Asparagus, avocado and pink grapefruit salad

CARROT SALAD WITH YOGHURT AND REDCURRANTS

(to replace minerals)

Serves 4

1 bunch long radishes

175 g/6 oz baby carrots

4 sticks celery

1 small lettuce

1 clove garlic

vinegar flavoured with redcurrants

extra virgin olive oil

400 ml/14 fl oz/1¾ cups goat's yoghurt

1 punnet redcurrants

salt (or substitute)

Trim and rinse the vegetables. Make deep, lengthwise cuts in the radishes and immerse in ice-cold water until they open like flowers. Blanch the carrots in boiling water for a couple of minutes, then drain. Chop the celery. Place a few lettuce leaves, carrots, radishes and celery slices on each plate. Crush the garlic and mix with 2 tbsp vinegar and 4 tbsp oil. Pour the vinaigrette over the vegetables, place a few tbsp yoghurt in the center and garnish with the redcurrants. Season with salt if desired.

ASPARAGUS, AVOCADO AND PINK GRAPEFRUIT SALAD

(liver-strengthening)

Serves 4

800 g/1¾ lb tender young asparagus

2 pink grapefruit

1 avocado

juice of 2 lemons

300 g/10 oz low fat cheese

1 bunch chervil

1 tbsp pistachio nuts, shelled and peeled

extra virgin olive oil

salt (or substitute)

Trim the woody ends from the asparagus; tie the tips in a bundle and cook upright in a tall pan only one third full of boiling water. Drain as soon as the tips are tender and leave to cool. Peel the grapefruit, removing all the pith, and slice thinly. Peel the avocado, discarding the stone, and cut into pieces. Sprinkle with lemon juice to avoid discoloration. Dice the cheese. Arrange all the ingredients on individual plates and garnish with chervil and chopped pistachio nuts. Serve with a simple dressing of oil and lemon juice.

LEEK, APPLE AND ALMOND SALAD

(to cleanse the complexion)

Serves 4

few leaves variegated lettuce

2 leeks

½ small Savoy cabbage

2 red apples

1 bunch parsley

1 tbsp shelled almonds

cider vinegar

extra virgin olive oil

1 bunch chervil

salt (or substitute)

Rinse the lettuce and other vegetables. Blanch the leek for 2 minutes in a little boiling water. Drain and slice (or serve raw, if preferred). Shred the cabbage. Rinse and dry the apples, remove the core, then slice thinly without peeling. Arrange all the ingredients on individual plates and garnish with parsley and sliced almonds. Prepare a dressing

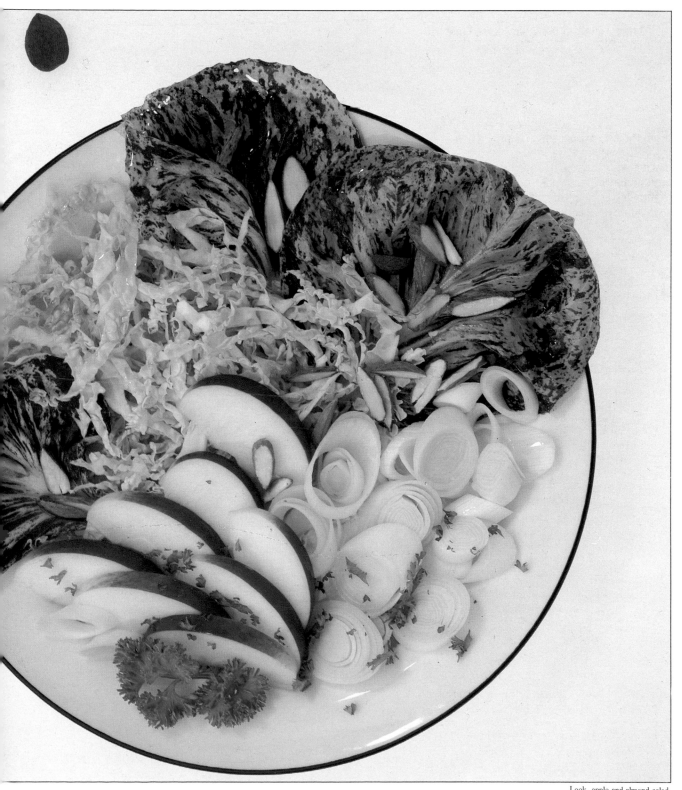

Leek, apple and almond salad

by mixing together 3 tbsp vinegar, 6 tbsp olive oil and the finely chopped chervil. Add salt if desired, and pour over the salad.

COTTAGE CHEESE SALAD WITH FRUIT

(fitness salad)

Serves 4

2 small heads red lettuce

2 oranges

2 slices fresh pineapple

2 tbsp sultanas (seedless white raisins)

salt (or substitute)

powdered onion

extra virgin olive oil

1 tbsp lemon juice

1 tbsp pumpkin seeds

400 g/14 oz cottage cheese

Rinse and dry the lettuce and arrange around the edge of each plate. Peel the oranges, then remove the thin skin from each segment. Cut the oranges and pineapple into pieces, then place in a bowl with the cottage cheese and sultanas (seedless white raisins). Sprinkle with salt and a generous amount of powdered onion, then pour over a thin trickle of oil and lemon juice. Spoon the fruit and cheese into the center of each plate and garnish with a few pumpkin seeds.

RADISH AND ALFALFA SALAD

(for a healthy respiratory system)

Serves 4

2 bunches radishes

4 carrots

1 lettuce

1 carton alfalfa

1 salsify

1 bunch fresh mint

extra virgin olive oil

white wine vinegar

salt (or substitute)

Rinse and trim all the vegetables: cut the radishes into thick slices, then into matchsticks. Slice the carrots obliquely into oval rings. Blanch for 1 minute in boiling water, or serve raw if preferred. Arrange the lettuce, carrots and radishes on individual plates, with a little alfalfa in the center of each. Peel and dice the salsify, then mix with the chopped mint, 4 tbsp oil and vinegar as desired. Pour the dressing over the salad and serve.

POTATO AND LEEK SALAD

(for special diets)

Serves 4

600 g/1¼ lb potatoes

3 turnips

2 leeks

2 Rennet apples

1 bunch fresh herbs (basil, parsley, mint, chervil, chives)

vinegar flavoured with cherries

extra virgin olive oil

salt substitute (optional)

Scrub the potatoes thoroughly to remove any earth, then cook in unsalted boiling water for 15–20 minutes or until tender. Leave to cool, then cut into rings without peeling. Prepare the turnips in the same way, then dice. Slice the leeks and blanch for 1

Radish and alfalfa salad

minute in the boiling water. Rinse the apples, remove the core, then dice them but do not peel. Arrange the drained vegetables and apple on individual plates, then prepare a vinaigrette by mixing together a few chopped fresh herbs, 3 tbsp vinegar and 1 tbsp oil per person. This already highly flavoured dressing should not require any salt.

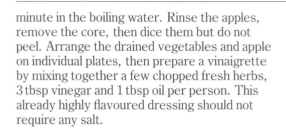

PRICKLY PEAR, PAPAYA AND RICOTTA SALAD

(to eliminate toxins)

Serves 4

2 prickly pears

1 large papaya

2 oranges or tangerines

125 g/4 oz/½ cup arbutus (strawberry tree) fruits

125 ml/4 fl oz/½ cup clear honey

400 g/14 oz ricotta cheese

1 lettuce heart

prickly pear, papaya and ricotta salad

Carefully peel the prickly pears, holding them in a cloth to avoid the spines. Peel the papaya, discard the seeds and cut the flesh into slices or decorative leaf shapes. Rinse and dry the oranges or tangerines and cut into wedges, but do not peel. Rinse and carefully dry the arbutus fruits. Mix the juice collected while preparing the fruit with the honey. Arrange a few lettuce leaves and a selection of fruit on each plate; place a portion of ricotta in the center and pour over the honey just before serving.

———

MELON AND PEAR SALAD WITH LEMON BALM

(for anaemics)
Serves 4
1 bunch watercress
1 small Cantaloupe melon
2 pears
2 marigold flowers
1 bunch wild thyme
1 bunch lemon balm
vinegar flavoured with lemon
extra virgin olive oil
salt

Rinse and dry the watercress and arrange on individual plates. Cut the melon in half, discard the seeds; peel, then cut into dice. Rinse the pears; cut in half and remove the core, then slice but do not peel. Place the fruit with the watercress then garnish each dish with the leaves and flowers of the marigolds. Finely chop the thyme and lemon balm and add to a dressing made with 3 tbsp vinegar and 6 tbsp oil. Season with salt and pour over the salad.

———

WATERCRESS AND GRAPE SALAD

(diuretic salad)
Serves 4
1 bunch dandelion leaves
1 bunch watercress
1 lettuce
1 bunch white grapes
2 tbsp leek juice
vinegar flavoured with bay leaf

extra virgin olive oil

salt substitute

Rinse and thoroughly dry the dandelion leaves, which should ideally be freshly picked. Rinse and dry the watercress and lettuce and place a few leaves on each plate with the dandelion leaves, and a few seeded grapes in the center. Prepare a vinaigrette by mixing together the leek juice, 3 tbsp vinegar and 6 tbsp oil. Beat vigorously with a whisk, then pour the dressing over the salad. Use only salt substitute in this salad, as sodium (in normal salt) is the main element responsible for water retention in the body.

FRENCH BEAN SALAD WITH PINE NUTS AND YEAST

(for cleansing the system)

Serves 4

400 g/14 oz French beans

1 small cucumber

2 red onions

few lettuce leaves

1–2 tbsp toasted pine nuts

50 g/2 oz fresh yeast

white wine vinegar

extra virgin olive oil

salt (or substitute)

Rinse the beans but do not trim them. Cook until tender in very little boiling water, then drain. Score the skin of the cucumber with a lemon zester, reserving the peel. Peel and finely slice the onions. Rinse and dry the lettuce and place a few leaves on each plate with half the finely sliced cucumber, the beans and the onions. Sprinkle with pine nuts and a little crumbled fresh yeast. Place the remaining half cucumber in a muslin cloth and

squeeze to extract the juice. Mix with 2 tbsp vinegar and 5 tbsp oil, then add the reserved chopped cucumber peel. Add salt if desired and pour the dressing over the salad.

CARROT AND BEETROOT SALAD WITH TARRAGON

(to restore the appetite)

Serves 4

2 carrots

1 raw beetroot

½ spring cabbage

2 tbsp shelled almonds

2 tbsp wheatgerm

1 bunch tarragon

walnut oil

white wine vinegar

salt

Rinse and trim the carrots and beetroot and grate both finely. Rinse the cabbage and slice finely. Arrange the three vegetables on individual plates without mixing them together, then sprinkle with the chopped almonds and wheatgerm and chopped tarragon. Make a vinaigrette with the walnut oil and vinegar and season with salt if desired.

CELERY, PEACH AND APPLE SALAD

(to combat high blood pressure)

Serves 4

4 sticks celery

1 large lettuce

2 Granny Smith apples

2 peaches

1 handful celery leaves

marjoram, lemon balm, thyme, sage

red wine vinegar

extra virgin olive oil

salt (or substitute)

Chop the celery. Rinse and drain the lettuce; leave the smaller leaves whole and tear the larger into pieces. Remove the core from the apples and the stone from the peaches and slice the fruit but do not peel. Arrange in individual dishes on top of the lettuce and celery. Chop the fresh herbs finely and add to a vinaigrette made with 3 tbsp vinegar and 6 tbsp oil. Season with salt if desired and pour the dressing over the salad.

———

SPINACH SALAD WITH PUMPKIN

(energy-giving)

Serves 4

300 g/10 oz pumpkin

5 Jerusalem artichokes

cider vinegar

150 g/5 oz fresh young spinach leaves

1 lettuce heart

150 g/5 oz cooked, shelled peas

225 g/8 oz/2 cups sweetcorn

1 bunch parsley

extra virgin olive oil

salt (or substitute)

Peel the pumpkin, cut into pieces and cook in boiling water for 5 minutes. Peel the Jerusalem artichokes and cook for 5–6 minutes in boiling water acidulated

with 1 tbsp vinegar. Rinse the spinach very thoroughly, then dry and arrange on individual plates with the lettuce, peas, sweetcorn, drained pumpkin and sliced artichokes. Sprinkle with coarsely chopped parsley. Make a vinaigrette by mixing together 3 tbsp vinegar, 6 tbsp olive oil and a little salt, if desired. Pour the dressing over the salad.

———

ARTICHOKE SALAD WITH SUNFLOWER SEEDS

(anti-cholesterol)

Serves 4

4 artichokes

juice of 1 lemon

1 lettuce heart

150 g/5 oz/¾ cup cooked soybeans

225 g/8 oz/2 cups sweetcorn

4 tsp sunflower seeds, shelled and toasted

salt (or substitute)

white wine vinegar

sunflower oil

Cook the artichokes in boiling salted water for 40–45 minutes. Drain, remove the leaves and the hairy choke. Slice the artichoke bottoms (*fonds*) finely and immerse in water acidulated with lemon juice. Rinse and dry the lettuce and arrange a few leaves around the edge of individual plates. Place a few soybeans, sweetcorn and drained artichoke slices in separate mounds on each plate and sprinkle with toasted sunflower seeds. Season with salt, vinegar and sunflower oil.

———

Spinach salad with pumpkin

ELEGANT SALADS

Probably the most significant changes in the world of cooking over the last few years have been brought about by the diffusion of *nouvelle cuisine*. This form of cooking evolved as the result of a universally felt need to adapt eating habits to new beliefs about the nutritional and aesthetic values of food. It has been acclaimed all over the world and while no longer strictly in the vanguard of fashion, its basic precepts continue to be relevant. Salads lend themselves well to the *nouvelle cuisine* philosophy that dishes, as well as tasting good, should be attractive to look at and easy to digest. This section seeks to create some elegant and unusual recipes for dinner party salads that will appeal to the eye as well as the palate. Luxury ingredients such as salmon, caviar, lobster and truffles are presented to maximum visual effect and are guaranteed to impress and please your guests.

SCALLOP SALAD

Serves 4

20 large scallops

butter

salt and freshly ground white pepper

2–3 tbsp dry vermouth

1 clementine

2 tbsp mayonnaise

150 ml/5 fl oz/¾ cup double (heavy) cream

juice of ½ lemon

1 bunch tarragon

50 g/2 oz lamb's lettuce, batavia or similar

1 heart frisée lettuce

Prise the scallop shells open and use a sharp knife to remove the meat. Rinse under cold running water and discard everything except the red coral and white cushion. Melt a little butter in a frying pan and gently fry the scallops for a few minutes on each side. Pour off the cooking liquor. Season the scallops with salt and pepper and sprinkle over the vermouth. Grate the clementine peel into strips and reserve; squeeze the juice. Mix together in a small bowl the mayonnaise, cream, lemon and clementine juice; add chopped tarragon to taste and season with salt and pepper. Place some frisée in the center of each plate with the lamb's lettuce arranged round it like the spokes of a wheel. Place 5 scallops on each plate and top with a spoonful of the cream sauce. Garnish with strips of clementine peel, and serve the remaining sauce separately.

On the previous page:
Scallop salad

Quail's egg and caviar salad

QUAIL'S EGG AND CAVIAR SALAD

Serves 4

12 hard-boiled quails' eggs

batavia lettuce

lemon juice

extra virgin olive oil

salt and freshly ground white pepper

50 g/2 oz caviar or black lumpfish roe

few chives

Shell the eggs and cut in half. Make a dressing with 1 tbsp lemon juice, 2 tbsp oil and a pinch of salt and pepper. Arrange a circle of batavia leaves around each plate (see illustration on page 107) and sprinkle with a little lemon dressing. Place a halved quail egg and a little caviar beside each leaf and garnish with whole chives as shown. Place a lettuce leaf, halved egg and some caviar in the center of each plate. Serve with thin slices of toasted bread.

ARITICHOKE SALAD WITH SOUR CREAM DRESSING

Serves 4

12 tender young artichokes

lemon juice

200 ml/7 fl oz/1 cup double (heavy) cream

juice of ½ pink grapefruit

salt and freshly ground black pepper

1 bunch lemon balm

Trim off all the leaves from the artichokes; remove the hairy choke. Plunge the artichoke bottoms (fonds) immediately into cold water acidulated with lemon juice to prevent discoloration. Mix the cream with 1 tbsp lemon juice and leave to stand in a warm place for 1 hour. Heat the grapefruit juice in a small saucepan until reduced to 2 tbsp, then stir into the cream. Season with salt and pepper, add the chopped lemon balm and leave to chill in the refrigerator. Cook the artichoke bottoms in boiling salted water with 2 tbsp lemon juice until tender. Drain and serve hot or cold with the sour cream dressing.

LOBSTER SALAD WITH SPICY TOMATO DRESSING

Serves 4

2 carrots

175 g/6 oz mange tout (snow peas)

175 g/6 oz fine green beans

20 young asparagus tips

4 ripe tomatoes

1 spring onion (scallion)

salt and freshly ground black pepper

1 clove garlic

extra virgin olive oil

chilli powder

2 cooked lobsters

Trim the vegetables. Cut the carrots into small decorative pieces, then cook all the vegetables in a steamer until tender but still crisp. Heat the tomatoes in the steamer for 2 minutes, then remove and discard the skin and seeds and chop coarsely. Finely chop the green part of the spring onion (scallion), then sprinkle over the tomatoes with a little crushed garlic, salt and pepper, 5 tbsp oil and a pinch of chilli powder. Leave to stand for at least 30 minutes. Break off the lobster claws and extract the meat, shell the tails and cut into slices. Arrange the lobster on individual plates with a selection of steamed vegetables and a little tomato dressing.

Lobster salad with spicy tomato dressing

Foie gras salad with radicchio
and redcurrants

WALDORF SALAD

Serves 4

150 ml/5 fl oz/⅔ cup natural yoghurt

150 ml/5 fl oz/⅔ cup mayonnaise

salt and freshly ground black pepper

2 red apples

4 sticks celery

2 tbsp chopped walnuts

1 tbsp chopped chives

Mix the yoghurt and mayonnaise together and season with salt and pepper. Peel and core the apples, then cut into dice. Mix with the yoghurt and mayonnaise immediately to prevent discoloration, then add the sliced celery and walnuts. Transfer to a serving dish and garnish with chopped chives.

FOIE GRAS SALAD WITH RADICCHIO AND REDCURRANTS

Serves 4

1 head radicchio

1 bunch watercress

vinegar flavoured with redcurrants

walnut oil

salt and freshly ground white pepper

fresh dill

1 punnet redcurrants

225 g/8 oz pâté de foie gras

Trim, rinse and dry the radicchio and watercress. Make a dressing with 2 tbsp vinegar, 4 tbsp walnut oil, salt and pepper, and leave to stand for at least 30 minutes in a cup containing a sprig of fresh dill.

Rinse and dry the redcurrants. Dip 2 spoons in hot water, then use to shape the pâté de foie gras into 12 oval portions. Place 3 on each plate and arrange radicchio leaves and redcurrants in between, with some watercress in the center. Pour a little dressing over the salad and garnish the foie gras with fresh dill. Serve with thinly sliced toasted bread.

GRAVLAX WITH ROCKET

Serves 4

black peppercorns

4 tbsp chopped dill

2 tbsp clear honey

salt

2 salmon fillets (800 g/1¾ lb)

2 bunches rocket

4 tbsp sour cream

2 tbsp mustard

white wine vinegar

extra virgin olive oil

Using a pestle and mortar pound together 1 tbsp black peppercorns, 2 tbsp chopped dill, the honey and 2 tbsp salt. Spread half the mixture over the bottom of a serving dish and place a salmon fillet on top. Cover with the remaining mixture and the second fillet. Cover with foil and place a weight on top, then leave to stand in the refrigerator for 2–3 days, turning the salmon carefully once a day. To serve, scrape off the marinade mixture and slice the salmon very thinly. Arrange on individual plates, with a little finely sliced rocket in the center. Mix together in a small bowl the sour cream, mustard, 2 tbsp vinegar, 4 tbsp oil, 2 tbsp chopped dill, salt and freshly ground black pepper. Serve the sauce separately.

SMOKED EEL SALAD

Serves 4

16 small fillets smoked eel

2 lemons

extra virgin olive oil

½ tbsp dry green peppercorns

1 large carrot

1 large courgette (zucchini)

salt and freshly ground black pepper

Place the eel fillets in a shallow dish and sprinkle with 2 tbsp lemon juice, 3 tbsp oil and the crushed green peppercorns. Leave to marinate for 1 hour. Peel the carrot; rinse the courgette (zucchini) and cut the vegetables into thin slices, then matchsticks. Mix together in a small bowl a generous pinch of salt, a pinch of black pepper, 2 tbsp lemon juice, and 4 tbsp oil. Pour the vinaigrette over the vegetables. Place the drained eel fillets on to a very hot grill (or barbecue) for a few seconds only until scored. Place a bed of vegetable strips on each plate and arrange 4 eel fillets on top, as illustrated below. Garnish with thin slices of lemon.

Smoked eel salad

SCAMPI SALAD WITH CANNELLINI BEANS

Serves 4

2 spring onions (scallions)

extra virgin olive oil

24 whole Dublin Bay prawns (scampi)

red wine vinegar

salt and freshly ground allspice

125 g/4 oz lamb's lettuce

300 g/10 oz/1½ cups cooked cannellini beans

2 tbsp chopped parsley

Chop the spring onions (scallions) and place in a large frying pan with 6 tbsp oil. When the oil is hot add the scampi and cook over high heat for 5 minutes. Meanwhile, heat 5 tbsp vinegar in a small saucepan until reduced by half, then pour over the scampi. Season with salt and plenty of allspice. Rinse and dry the lettuce and mix with the beans. Shell 20 scampi, reserving the cooking liquor; cut in half and add to the salad. Pour over the reserved liquor, sprinkle with chopped parsley and adjust the seasoning. Serve on individual plates and garnish with the remaining whole scampi.

TRUFFLE SALAD WITH PARMESAN AND CELERY

Serves 4

1 white truffle (about 50 g/2 oz)

2 heads celery

125 g/4 oz Parmesan cheese (in one piece)

salt and freshly ground black pepper

extra virgin olive oil

Brush the truffle carefully to remove any earth. If necessary rub

gently with a cloth soaked in white wine. Remove and discard the hard outer celery stalks. Finely slice the tender inner sticks. Cut the Parmesan into thin flakes and mix both ingredients together in a bowl. Sprinkle with salt, plenty of pepper and the finest quality olive oil. Transfer the salad to individual plates and when the guests are already seated, sprinkle each serving with a layer of finely sliced truffle.

PARMA HAM WITH RUBY SALAD

Serves 4

1 head radicchio

2 heads chicory (Belgian endive)

¼ pickled red pepper

1 tbsp raspberry or strawberry vinegar

mild paprika

salt and freshly ground black pepper

3 tbsp whipped cream

125 ml/4 fl oz/½ cup mayonnaise

12 slices Parma ham

1 slice watermelon

Rinse and dry the radicchio and chicory (Belgian endive), then chop coarsely. Coarsely chop the red pepper. Mix the vinegar, a pinch of paprika, a pinch of pepper and the whipped cream into the mayonnaise, then stir in the chopped salad ingredients. Add salt if necessary. Twist the 12 slices of Parma ham into cones and fill with the salad mixture. Place on a serving dish and garnish with balls of watermelon, cut out using a melon baller. Chill in the refrigerator until ready to serve.

SALMON SALAD MOULDS

Serves 4

1 carrot

1 stick celery

1 small leek

1 onion

400 ml/14 fl oz/1¾ cups dry white wine

1 bay leaf

1 clove

few peppercorns

4 small courgettes (zucchini)

200 g/7 oz broccoli

4 salmon steaks

1 bunch parsley

few sorrel leaves

2–3 tbsp brandy

1 sachet gelatine

4 small tomatoes

1 heart frisée lettuce

extra virgin olive oil

1 tbsp lemon juice

strawberry vinegar

salt and freshly ground black pepper

Peel or trim the carrot, celery, leek and onion. Chop coarsely and place in a saucepan with ¾ liter/1¼ pints/3 cups water, the white wine, bay leaf, clove and a few peppercorns. Bring slowly to the boil and simmer the court bouillon for 20 minutes. Strain, season lightly with salt, and cook the courgettes (zucchini) and broccoli in the court bouillon until tender. Remove with a slotted spoon; cut the courgettes (zucchini) into oblique slices and the broccoli florets in half. Poach the salmon gently in the court bouillon for 10 minutes. Drain, remove any bones and skin, then flake into chunks. Rinse and dry the parsley and sorrel; chop finely and sprinkle over the salmon, stirring carefully until it is completely covered. Strain the court bouillon through a fine muslin cloth, return to the heat until reduced to 400 ml/14 fl oz/1¾ cups, then add the cognac. Allow the alcohol to evaporate, then leave to cool. Prepare the gelatine according to the manufacturer's instructions, using the court bouillon as the liquid. While it is still warm, pour a little into the bottom of 4 individual moulds and place in the refrigerator for 5 minutes. Remove from the refrigerator and distribute the salmon and herbs between the moulds. Cover with the remaining gelatine and return to the refrigerator to set. To unmould, dip briefly in hot water, then place the salmon moulds on 4 individual plates. Surround each serving with a selection of vegetables, tomato wedges and frisée lettuce. Dress with a vinaigrette made with oil, lemon juice, vinegar, salt and pepper.

MUSHROOM SALAD

Serves 4

600 g/1¼ lb mushrooms

125 g/4 oz Parmesan cheese (in one piece)

lemon juice

extra virgin olive oil

salt and freshly ground white pepper

Clean the mushrooms carefully, removing any earth with a damp cloth. Slice finely, then cut the Parmesan into thin flakes with a special cheese cutter. Arrange on individual plates and before serving dress with a vinaigrette made with 2 tbsp lemon juice, 5 tbsp oil, salt and pepper. Mix carefully.

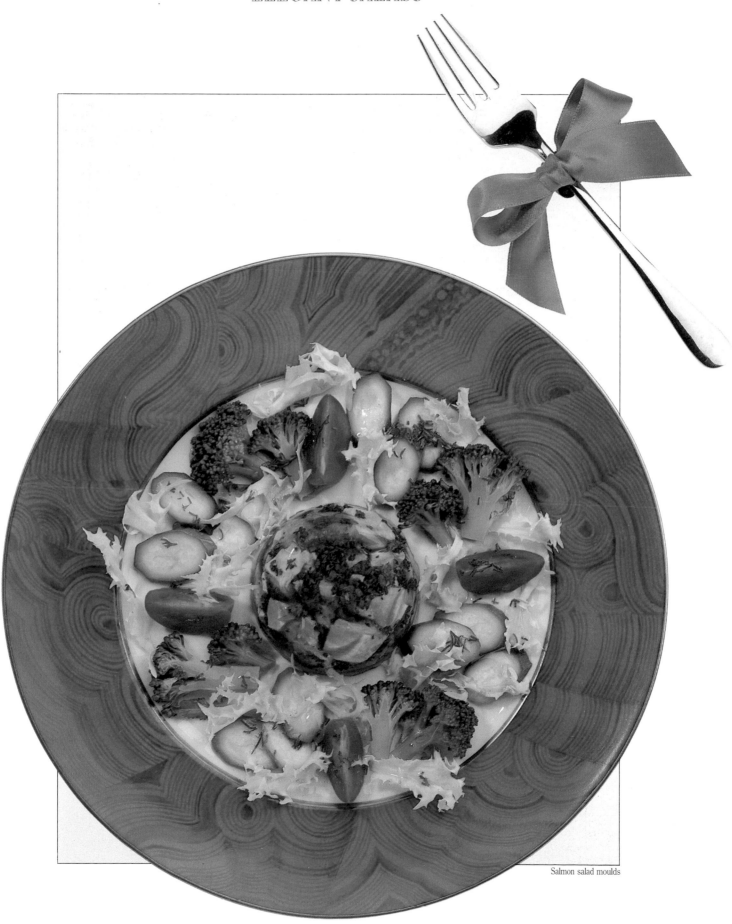

Salmon salad moulds

CREATIVE SALADS

Salads can be a very creative area of cuisine, offering wide scope to the cook's imagination. Experiment with different combinations of colour and flavour, cut certain ingredients into decorative shapes, and aim where possible for a contrast in texture: the addition of nuts, celery or other crunchy ingredients can provide interesting detail. Be adventurous in your choice of ingredients and dressings, and inventive in your presentation. Garnishes can also play a creative part, elevating a salad on to a more sophisticated level: a sprinkling of toasted almonds or pine nuts, chopped or whole herbs, wedges of citrus fruit (or strips of peel) are just a few suggestions. The possibilities are endless.

With a little attention to detail, it is easy to create aesthetically pleasing salads, that are fun to assemble and impressive enough to serve when entertaining.

On the previous page:
Salmon salad with anchovy
dressing

WARM CHICKEN LIVER AND RASPBERRY SALAD

Serves 4

225 g/8 oz mixed lettuce (e.g. lamb's lettuce, batavia, *feuille de chêne*)

225 g/8 oz raspberries

16 chicken livers

salt

butter

5–6 tbsp sherry

1 tsp pink peppercorns, crushed

raspberry vinegar

extra virgin olive oil

Distribute the lettuce and raspberries between four plates. Rinse the chicken livers and pat dry. Using a sharp knife remove any fat and green parts, then sprinkle lightly with salt. Melt 2 tbsp butter in a large frying pan and sauté the livers for 5 minutes. Drain off the cooking liquid, return the pan to the heat and add the sherry and crushed pink peppercorns. Cook for a further 2–3 minutes, then remove the livers and keep warm. Add 4 tbsp vinegar to the pan and stir over heat into the pan juices. Strain through a fine sieve into a bowl, then beat in 4 tbsp oil with a whisk. Cut the chicken livers in half, add to the salad and pour over the warm dressing. Serve immediately.

SALMON SALAD WITH ANCHOVY DRESSING

Serves 4

¼ yellow pepper

¼ red pepper

2 sticks celery

1 frisée lettuce

Warm chicken liver
and raspberry salad

400 g/14 oz salmon

salt and freshly ground black pepper

juice of 1 lemon

2 carrots

2 courgettes (zucchini)

½ clove garlic

anchovy paste

extra virgin olive oil

Trim and rinse all the vegetables and cut the peppers into small triangles. Slice the celery obliquely into long diagonal pieces. Tear the lettuce. Poach the salmon for 10 minutes in lightly salted boiling water then drain. Discard the skin and bones, flake, and season with pepper and a little lemon juice. Cut the carrots and courgettes (zucchini) into long strips, then blanch for 2–3 minutes in boiling water. Drain them and lay a few on each dish in a lattice pattern (see illustration on page 117). Crush the garlic and mix with ½ tsp anchovy paste. Gradually work in the lemon juice and 5 tbsp oil. Place the lettuce, peppers, celery and salmon in a large bowl and pour over the anchovy dressing. Mix carefully and distribute between the four plates.

—

GOAT'S CHEESE AND GRAPE SALAD

Serves 4

300 g/10 oz soft goat's cheese

salt and freshly ground black pepper

tabasco

mild paprika

2 hearts escarole lettuce

2 tbsp flaked almonds

4 small bunches red grapes

strawberry vinegar

extra virgin olive oil

Mash the goat's cheese and work in 2 pinches of pepper, 2 pinches of salt and a few drops of tabasco. Shape the cheese into balls the size of grapes and sprinkle with mild paprika. Place in the refrigerator. Rinse and dry the lettuce and tear into pieces. Toast the almonds lightly under the grill. Rinse and dry the grapes. Mix 2 tbsp vinegar with 4 tbsp oil and season with salt and pepper. Pour the vinaigrette over the lettuce and distribute between four plates. Place a bunch of grapes on each plate, substituting one or two grapes with balls of cheese (see illustration). Arrange the remaining cheese balls and grapes on the bed of lettuce and sprinkle with toasted almonds.

Note: If goat's cheese is not to your taste, substitute cream cheese.

———

PEAR AND TUNA SALAD

Serves 4
125 g/4 oz lamb's lettuce
4 Williams pears
400 g/14 oz tuna
juice of 2 lemons
4 tbsp extra virgin olive oil

Goat's cheese and grape salad

1 tbsp chopped parsley

½ tbsp chopped chives

salt

Rinse and trim the lettuce, then dry carefully, avoiding tearing the delicate leaves. Rinse the pears, discard the core and cut into dice. Flake the tuna fish with a fork and mix together with the pears in a bowl. Season with the lemon juice and oil, then sprinkle with the chopped herbs and a little salt. Before serving mix with the lamb's lettuce and transfer to four individual plates.

PEAR AND AVOCADO SALAD

Serves 4

1 heart escarole lettuce

200 g/7 oz mild white cheese (e.g. white Stilton, Wensleydale)

white wine vinegar

extra virgin olive oil

salt and freshly ground pepper

2 red Williams pears

1 avocado

juice of 1 lemon

16 slices Parma ham

Trim and rinse the lettuce and tear into pieces. Cut the cheese into small wedges. Make a vinaigrette with 1 tbsp vinegar, 3 tbsp oil, salt and pepper. Rinse the pears and cut them in half. Remove the cores and slice the pears finely. Peel the avocado, remove the stone and slice the flesh finely. Sprinkle both the pears and avocado with lemon juice to prevent discoloration. Cover each plate with 4 slices of Parma ham. Pour the dressing over the lettuce and cheese and place a little in the corner of each plate. Arrange alternate slices of pear and avocado around the ham in a fan shape, as illustrated on page 123.

QUAIL'S EGG AND CHEESE SALAD

Serves 4

32 quails' eggs

150 g/5 oz lamb's lettuce

125 g/4 oz Parmesan cheese (in one piece)

salt and freshly ground black pepper

juice of 1 lemon

extra virgin olive oil

Place the eggs in a saucepan; cover with cold water and bring to the boil. One minute after the water has started to boil, remove the saucepan from the heat and place the eggs under cold running water. Shell the eggs and leave to cool. Trim and rinse the lettuce; dry carefully, avoiding tearing the leaves. Arrange on individual plates and cover with the sliced eggs and wafer-thin pieces of cheese. Season with salt and pepper, lemon juice and oil.

RAZOR CLAM AND MINT SALAD

Serves 4

1 kg/2¼ lb razor clams

250 ml/9 fl oz/generous 1 cup dry white wine

1 bunch mint

salt and freshly ground black pepper

juice of 2 lemons

1 clove garlic

3 small spring onions (scallions)

extra virgin olive oil

1 small lettuce

Scrub the razor clams clean and leave under cold running water for a few hours. Drain and place in a large saucepan

Smoked cheese salad with fennel dressing

with the wine and half the mint. Place over high heat until the shells open. (Discard any that remain closed.) Remove the meat from the shells and transfer to a bowl; sprinkle with pepper, lemon juice, chopped garlic and spring onions (scallions); add the remaining mint cut finely with scissors, and plenty of oil. Rinse and dry the lettuce, tearing the larger leaves into pieces, and arrange on individual plates. Cover with the razor clams and serve.

MIXED PEPPER SALAD

Serves 4
1 yellow pepper
1 red pepper
1 green pepper
extra virgin olive oil
1½ tbsp sultanas (seedless white raisins)
1 tbsp pine nuts
2 tbsp fresh breadcrumbs
2 bunches rocket or watercress
salt and freshly ground black pepper
red wine vinegar

Remove the core and seeds from the peppers and cut them into strips. Heat 6 tbsp oil in a large frying pan and sauté the pepper strips for 3–4 minutes. Remove with a slotted spoon and keep warm. Add the sultanas (seedless white raisins) and pine nuts to the frying pan and sauté briefly. Remove with a slotted spoon and place with the peppers. Add 1 tbsp fresh oil to the frying pan and brown the breadcrumbs. Meanwhile, trim and rinse the rocket, tear into pieces and add to the peppers. Season with salt and pepper, sprinkle with 2 tbsp vinegar and the breadcrumbs, and serve warm.

SMOKED CHEESE SALAD WITH FENNEL DRESSING

Serves 4
1 tsp peppercorns
1 tbsp fennel seeds
1 bunch wild rocket (with long, tougher leaves)
red wine vinegar
extra virgin olive oil
salt
1 heart frisée lettuce
1 bunch cultivated rocket (short-leaved variety)
4 button mushrooms
125 g/4 oz smoked cheese

Place the peppercorns and fennel seeds in a mortar and, using a pestle, pound to a paste with 2 leaves wild rocket. Gradually add 3 tbsp vinegar and 7 tbsp oil; add salt to taste and mix well. Rinse all the salad ingredients; dry carefully and tear into pieces. Trim the mushrooms; remove any earth, then rinse and dry carefully. Slice thinly. Cut the cheese into wafer-thin slices, preferably with a special cheese-cutter. Place all the ingredients together in a large bowl and pour over the fennel dressing just before serving.
Note: If rocket is unavailable, substitute watercress.

SMOKED HAM AND PINEAPPLE SALAD

Serves 4

1 head radicchio

300 g/10 oz smoked ham

4 slices fresh pineapple

few tbsp pineapple juice

extra virgin olive oil

salt and freshly ground allspice

Rinse and dry the lettuce; tear the larger leaves into pieces and leave the smaller ones whole. Cut the ham into large dice or strips and the pineapple into chunks. Heat the pineapple juice in a saucepan until it becomes syrupy, then remove from the heat and add 3 tbsp sherry vinegar, 4 tbsp oil and a pinch of salt. Mix the lettuce, ham and pineapple together in a large bowl, pour over the dressing and sprinkle generously with ground allspice.

ORANGE AND MELON SALAD

Serves 4

1 head escarole lettuce

1 head chicory (Belgian endive)

2 oranges

½ clove garlic

4 tbsp mayonnaise

2 tbsp natural yoghurt

2 tbsp orange juice

Cayenne pepper

1 small green melon

2 tbsp sweetcorn

Rinse and dry the lettuce and chicory (Belgian endive) and tear

into pieces. Wash one orange and grate the rind. Set aside. Peel both oranges, removing all the pith. Crush the garlic and mix with the mayonnaise, yoghurt, orange juice, grated orange rind and a generous pinch of Cayenne pepper. Add three orange wedges, cut into chunks, and place the dressing in the refrigerator. Peel the melon, discard the seeds and cut the flesh into chunks. Mix together the orange, melon, sweetcorn, lettuce and chicory in a large bowl and serve with the chilled dressing.

CARAMELIZED POTATO AND ONION SALAD

Serves 4

extra virgin olive oil

300 g/10 oz peeled baby onions

400 g/14 oz new potatoes

salt and freshly ground white pepper

2 tbsp sugar

cider vinegar

1 sprig rosemary

Heat 4 tbsp oil in a large frying pan, add the onions and cook gently over low heat for 20 minutes, shaking the pan occasionally. Cook the potatoes in boiling, lightly salted water for 10–15 minutes or until tender. Drain, cool under cold water, then peel. Add them to the onions in the frying pan with a little extra oil if necessary. Turn up the heat, sprinkle with sugar and allow to caramelize. Add a few tbsp vinegar to soften the caramel, then remove the vegetables from the heat. Sprinkle with salt, pepper and freshly chopped rosemary and serve warm or cold.

Orange and melon salad

ANYTIME SALADS

This section is made up of a collection of recipes that do not appear to have anything in common. Some are based on traditional ingredients, others are a little more unexpected. When you are not sure what to serve, these salads provide the perfect solution, suitable for an informal meal with your family, a working lunch with colleagues where a full meal is not required, or perhaps an after-theater supper with friends. Fresh, light and easily digestible, these salads are attractive, easy to prepare and sure to please.

On the previous page:
Watercress and tomato
salad with goat's cheese

WATERCRESS AND TOMATO SALAD WITH GOAT'S CHEESE

Serves 4

2 bunches watercress

2 tomatoes

300 g/10 oz goat's cheese (e.g. bûche de chèvre)

20 black olives

1 bunch thyme

1 tsp tapénade (black olive paste)

red wine vinegar

extra virgin olive oil

salt and freshly ground black pepper

Trim the watercress; discard the larger leaves, reserving only the tender young leaves. Rinse and dry carefully. Rinse the tomatoes and slice thinly. Cut the goat's cheese into flakes. Place a ring of tomato slices around each plate with a little watercress and goat's cheese in the center. Garnish with olives and thyme. Mix the olive paste in a small bowl with 3 tbsp vinegar, 7 tbsp oil, salt, pepper and 1 tbsp thyme leaves. Beat well and pour the dressing over the salad just before serving.

—

SPINACH AND PARMESAN SALAD WITH ASPARAGUS DRESSING

Serves 4

300 g/10 oz tender young spinach leaves

20 asparagus tips (fresh, canned or frozen)

125 g/4 oz Parmesan cheese (in one piece)

2 tbsp pine nuts

2 eggs

150 ml/5 fl oz/⅔ cup double (heavy) cream

1 lemon

salt and freshly ground black pepper

Spinach and parmesan salad with asparagus dressing

Remove the stalks from the spinach and use only the tenderest leaves. Wash in several changes of cold water to remove all earth and grit. Drain and dry. If using fresh asparagus, trim and tie into a bundle with string. Cook in a tall saucepan in 5 cm (2 in) boiling water for 5–10 minutes until the tips are tender. Cut off the tips and set aside; return the stalks to the pan and cook until tender. Drain thoroughly and purée the stalks using a blender or vegetable mill. (If the purée is too watery, stir over heat for a few seconds). Cut the cheese into wafer-thin pieces and toast the pine nuts under the grill. Boil the eggs for 7 minutes; shell them and mash with a fork. Mix the asparagus purée with the cream, then add the juice and grated peel of ½ lemon. Season with salt and pepper. Whisk the sauce lightly and chill in the refrigerator. Mix together the spinach leaves, asparagus tips, cheese and pine nuts in a large bowl; sprinkle with the mashed hard-boiled eggs and serve the sauce separately. For a lighter dressing, mix 3 tbsp lemon juice, 6 tbsp extra virgin olive oil, salt, plenty of pepper and 2 tbsp asparagus purée.

MUSSEL SALAD

Serves 4

1.2 kg/2¾ lb mussels
125 ml/4 fl oz/½ cup dry white wine
1 small onion
1 bay leaf
2 lemons
extra virgin olive oil
salt and freshly ground black pepper
1 bunch parsley
125 g/4 oz French beans
2 young courgettes (zucchini)
225 g/8 oz lamb's lettuce

Scrub the mussels thoroughly under cold running water, using a stiff brush, and remove beards and barnacles. Discard any that do not close when tapped sharply. Place in a large uncovered saucepan over high heat for a few minutes until the shells begin to open. Discard any that do not . Pour off any water, then add the wine, finely chopped onion and the bay leaf to the pan. Heat for a few more minutes until the shells are completely opened. Remove the mussels from their shells and set aside. Strain the cooking liquor, return to the heat and reduce to 2 tbsp. Allow to cool, then mix with 3 tbsp lemon juice, 6 tbsp oil, pepper and 1 tbsp chopped parsley. Add salt if necessary. Trim and chop the beans. Peel the courgettes (zucchini) in alternate strips and cut into thick slices. Cook both vegetables in boiling lightly salted water for about 5 minutes, or until tender but still crisp. Trim the lamb's lettuce; rinse and dry carefully. Mix together in a large bowl the lettuce, beans, courgettes (zucchini), mussels and a handful of fresh parsley. Pour over the lemon dressing and mix carefully before serving.

COURGETTE (ZUCCHINI) AND MINT SALAD

Serves 4

10 young courgettes (zucchini)
extra virgin olive oil
1 tbsp lemon juice
salt and freshly ground black pepper
1 tbsp Dijon mustard
2 tbsp single (light) cream
150 ml/5 fl oz/⅔ cup natural yoghurt
1 bunch mint

Rinse and dry the courgettes (zucchini), cut off the ends and slice finely. Sprinkle with a little oil, lemon juice, salt and pepper. Mix together the mustard, cream, yoghurt, salt and pepper. Heat the sauce in a

Mussel salad

Mozzarella salad

bain marie or double saucepan, stirring constantly; remove from the heat when warm and transfer to a warm sauceboat. Sprinkle the courgettes (zucchini) with finely chopped mint and serve the sauce separately.

ROQUEFORT SALAD WITH PORT DRESSING

Serves 4
butter
1 clove garlic
2 tbsp chopped hazelnuts (filberts)
2 small lettuces
250 g/9 oz Roquefort cheese
1 tsp mustard
1 tbsp sherry vinegar
2 tbsp port
juice of ½ orange
extra virgin olive oil
salt and freshly ground black pepper

Melt 1 tbsp butter in a small saucepan and heat the peeled garlic clove for a few minutes. Remove the garlic and add the coarsely chopped hazelnuts (filberts). Allow to brown, stirring occasionally. Drain on kitchen paper. Rinse and dry the lettuces and arrange the best leaves around the edge of a serving dish. Tear the others into pieces, mix with the hazelnuts and place in the center of the dish. Crumble the cheese with a fork and add to the salad. Mix together the mustard, vinegar and port in a small bowl; whisk in the orange juice and 6 tbsp oil. Season with salt and pepper and pour the dressing over the salad just before serving.

MOZZARELLA SALAD

Serves 4
175 g/6 oz mixed lettuce
½ red pepper
1 courgette (zucchini)
salt and freshly ground black pepper
1 Mozzarella cheese (500 g/generous 1 lb)
2 tbsp capers
2 ripe tomatoes
red wine vinegar
extra virgin olive oil
1 tbsp dried oregano

Rinse the lettuce and dry thoroughly. Finely slice the red pepper. Cut the courgette (zucchini) into matchsticks and cook in lightly salted boiling water for 2–3 minutes. Drain and mix with the pepper and lettuce. Place a little mixed salad on half of four individual plates. On the other half place a few slices freshly cut Mozzarella cheese, and sprinkle with capers. Blanch the tomatoes for 2 minutes in boiling water; drain, peel them, cut them in half, discard the seeds, then chop coarsely. Sprinkle over the salad. Mix together 3 tbsp vinegar, 7 tbsp oil, salt, pepper and oregano. Pour the dressing over the salad just before serving.

Octopus salad

ARTICHOKE AND RADICCHIO SALAD WITH MUSTARD DRESSING

Serves 4

2 heads radicchio

4 artichokes

juice of 1 lemon

1½ tbsp Dijon mustard

salt and freshly ground black pepper

tarragon vinegar

extra virgin olive oil

2 tbsp double (heavy) cream (at room temperature)

Rinse and dry the radicchio; leave the center leaves whole and tear the larger ones into pieces. Arrange on a serving plate. Cook the artichokes in boiling salted water for 40–45 minutes. Drain, remove the leaves and the hairy choke. Slice the artichoke bottoms (*fonds*) finely and add to the radicchio. Make the dressing: mix together the mustard, 3 pinches of salt, a pinch of pepper and 1 tbsp vinegar in a small bowl. Using a wooden spoon, gradually work in 125 ml/4 fl oz/½ cup oil, pouring it in a very fine trickle. Stir in the cream, which must be at room temperature to avoid curdling. Pour the mustard dressing over the salad and serve.

OCTOPUS SALAD

Serves 4

1 kg/2¼ lb octopus

2 lemons

extra virgin olive oil

salt and mixed black and white pepper

1 bunch dill

1 head radicchio

2 small pink grapefruit

1 head red Treviso chicory

Rinse the octopus and place in an ovenproof dish with no water. Cook for 1–2 hours in a low oven (300°F/150°C/ mark 2.) The octopus will give out a red liquid. When tender (test with a knife) drain, and rinse under cold running water. Remove the skin and bosses. Cook the tentacles in boiling salted water for 10 minutes, drain and leave to cool. Slice the tentacles, place in a bowl, and sprinkle with the juice of 1 lemon, 2 tbsp oil, salt, white and black pepper and 1 tbsp chopped dill. Cover and leave to marinate for a few hours, stirring occasionally. Rinse and dry the radicchio and chicory, and finely slice the latter. Peel the grapefruit, reserving the juice, and taking care to remove all the pith, then peel each individual segment. Mix any grapefruit juice with 2 tbsp lemon juice, salt, pepper and 6 tbsp oil. Whisk well. Drain the octopus and mix with the sliced chicory and grapefruit. Pour over the dressing and distribute between four plates. Sprinkle with chopped dill and garnish with whole radicchio leaves.

MARINATED CHICKEN SALAD

Serves 4

| 2 carrots |
| 2 red onions |
| 2 sticks celery |
| ½ liter/18 fl oz/2¼ cups stock |
| 4 boneless chicken breasts |
| red wine vinegar |
| extra virgin olive oil |
| salt and freshly ground black pepper |
| 1 head Cos lettuce |
| 10 green olives |
| ½ tbsp fresh thyme |
| 1 bunch basil |

Peel the carrots and onions and trim the celery. Add the vegetables to the stock, bring to the boil and simmer for 10 minutes. Add the chicken breasts and simmer for a further 20 minutes or until the juices run clear. Remove with a slotted spoon, reserving the liquid, and leave to cool, then place in the refrigerator. Dice the carrots and celery. Rub the onions through a sieve (or purée in a food processor) and place in a saucepan with 6 tbsp stock. Reduce over high heat until the onion is quite dry, then add 5 tbsp vinegar. Allow half the vinegar to evaporate, then turn off the heat and leave to cool. Add 125 ml/4 fl oz/ ½ cup oil, salt and pepper. Make shallow, diagonal cuts in the chicken, then place in a shallow dish and sprinkle with the diced vegetables and onion marinade. Leave in the refrigerator for several hours, turning occasionally. Finely slice the lettuce and mix with the pitted and chopped olives, the thyme and basil. Distribute between four individual plates and place a chicken breast on each. Spoon some marinade over each serving.

PEACH SALAD WITH CHEESE AND WALNUTS

Serves 4

| 1 escarole lettuce |
| 1 frisée lettuce |
| 2 peaches |
| 225 g/8 oz Tilsiter (or Gruyère) cheese |
| 8 walnuts |
| 1½ tbsp sultanas (seedless white raisins) |
| white wine vinegar |
| walnut oil |
| salt and freshly ground black pepper |

Rinse and dry the lettuces and keep them separate. Arrange the escarole around the edges of four individual

Peach salad with cheese
and walnuts

plates and place the frisée in the center. Peel and finely slice the peaches. Cut the cheese into slices, then into matchsticks. Arrange peach slices, cheese strips, walnuts and sultanas (seedless white raisins) on each plate. Make a vinaigrette with 2 tbsp vinegar, 5 tbsp oil, salt and pepper; pour over the salad just before serving.

WARM MANGE TOUT (SNOW PEA) AND FRENCH BEAN SALAD

Serves 4

250 g/9 oz mange tout (snow peas)

250 g/9 oz French beans

extra virgin olive oil

few chives

1 bunch parsley

50 g/2 oz/¼ cup butter

juice of 1½ lemons

salt and freshly ground black pepper

Trim the mange tout (snow peas) and French beans, removing the ends and any stringy edges. Cook the beans in lightly salted boiling water until tender and the mange tout (snow peas) for 2 minutes. Drain the vegetables when tender but still crisp and sprinkle with a little oil. Rinse, dry and finely chop the chives and parsley. Melt the butter in a small saucepan. Holding the pan over the heat, gradually whisk in the lemon juice. Add the chopped chives and parsley, season with salt and pepper and pour over the vegetables. Serve at once.

PRAWN (SHRIMP) SALAD WITH FRUIT

Serves 4

150 ml/5 fl oz/⅔ cup mayonnaise

white wine vinegar

3 tbsp lemon juice

2 tbsp whipped cream

salt and freshly ground black pepper

1 lettuce

2 Rennet apples

1 grapefruit

1 banana

400 g/14 oz cooked prawn (shrimp) tails

Mix the mayonnaise with 2 tbsp vinegar and 1 tbsp lemon juice. Stir in the whipped cream carefully, using a spatula, and sprinkle generously with black pepper. Rinse and dry the lettuce; reserve the best leaves and tear the others into pieces. Rinse and quarter the apples, remove the core and cut them into slices. Peel the grapefruit, then peel each segment. Cut the banana into slices. Place all the fruit in a bowl and sprinkle with the remaining lemon juice. Shell the prawns (shrimp). Arrange the whole lettuce leaves on four individual plates. Place the remaining lettuce, the fruit and prawns (shrimp) in the center. Pour 1 tbsp dressing over each plate and serve the rest separately.

POACHED EGG SALAD

Serves 4

1 frisée lettuce

150 g/5 oz lamb's lettuce

4 slices white bread

125 g/4 oz/½ cup butter

2 egg yolks

3 tbsp dry white wine
lemon juice
salt and freshly ground black pepper
white wine vinegar
4 large eggs

Rinse and dry the lettuce and arrange on four individual plates. Cut the bread into dice and toast lightly under the grill. Prepare the sauce: melt the butter and allow to cool. In a double saucepan or bain marie beat together the egg yolks and white wine over moderate heat. When it begins to thicken gradually add the butter. Season with 1 tbsp lemon juice (or more, according to taste), salt and pepper. Keep the sauce warm over very low heat until required. Heat a large high-sided saucepan of water; as soon as it begins to boil, pour in 2 tbsp vinegar, lower the heat and move the saucepan slightly off the heat. Break an egg on to a saucer, then slide carefully into the boiling water. Remove with a slotted spoon as soon as the white is set. Poach the other eggs similarly, and when they are all cooked place an egg and a few toasted croûtons in the center of each plate. Spoon over 1 tbsp warm sauce and serve the rest separately.

ROAST BEEF ROULADES WITH VEGETABLE SALAD

Serves 4
125 ml/4 fl oz/½ cup mayonnaise
red wine vinegar
mild paprika
tabasco
milk
¼ red pepper
1 bunch chives
salt and freshly ground black pepper
150 g/50 oz new potatoes

150 g/5 oz baby carrots
125 g/4 oz cherry tomatoes
150 g/5 oz lamb's lettuce
12 thin slices cold roast beef

Prepare the sauce first: mix the mayonnaise with 1 tbsp vinegar, ½ tsp paprika, a few drops of tabasco, 2 tbsp milk, the finely chopped red pepper and 1 tbsp chopped chives. Season with salt and pepper and chill in the refrigerator until required. Scrub the potatoes thoroughly then cook in boiling salted water for 10 minutes or until tender. Drain and slice. Cook the carrots for 6–7 minutes. Rinse the tomatoes and cut in half. Rinse and dry the lettuce. Distribute the salad and vegetables between four plates. Spread ½ tbsp sauce on each slice of roast beef; roll up and tie with a whole chive. Place 3 beef roulades on each plate and serve the remaining sauce separately.

INDEX

INDEX

Acknowledgements

The publishers wish to thank the following companies for having supplied material for the photographs:

Bernardaud, Limoges
Co Mei Hing, Milan
Controbuffet, Milan
Croff, Milan
Koivu, Milan
La Rinascente, Milan
Penelopi 3, Milan
Puiforcat, Besozzi, Milan
Rede Guzzini